Acts

The Continuing Acts of Jesus in all the nations

First published 2009

ISBN No: 978-1-905975-20-4

Published by Biblical Frameworks

Reg. Office: 23 Coe Lane, Tarleton, Preston, PR4 6HH.

Cover design, typesetting and production management by
Verité CM Ltd, Worthing, West Sussex UK +44 (0) 1903 241975

Illustrations by Richard Thomas

Printed in England

Biblical Frameworks is registered in England No: 5712581
Charity No: 1116805.

Contents

Paul and Barnabas

I. Introductory thoughts from Paul Blackham

The longest chapter in the Bible is all about... the Bible! Psalm 119 is all about the wonder of the Word of God. Verse 103 shows us the heart of someone who really loved the Bible. He cries out to the LORD God:

Psalm 119:103 – "How sweet are your words to my taste, sweeter than honey to my mouth!"

Whether you are reading the Bible alone or in some kind of group with others, expect to be thrilled by the words of the Living God. This is not like reading any other book. When we read and study the Bible the ultimate Author can be present with you, showing you His words and applying them to you.

Thousands of small groups are starting up all over the world – but what is it that is going to sustain them? It has to be the Bible.

So often, people don't quite know what to do with these small groups. Meeting together, sharing testimonies and experiences or sharing the odd verse is ultimately too sparse a diet to sustain people's spiritual needs in the long run, and really help them to grow.

What is needed is confidence in the Bible, and the ability to go to a *book* of the Bible rather than just an isolated verse. Each book of the Bible was written with a purpose, and it is only as we digest it as a book that we understand the real message, purpose, direction, storyline and characters.

It's a lot easier than people often think. You might think, "Oh, I can't manage a whole book of the Bible", but what we're trying to do in Book by Book is to break it down and show that it's easy.

The Bible was written not for specialists, not for academics – it was written for the regular believers, down the ages.

The world is in desperate need for answers. How can the world live at peace? How can we live together with justice and truth and compassion? There are so many religions and so much division and bloodshed: what is the real and living way that takes us to the Living God who can give us all a new beginning?

The Bible is the answer of the Living God to all our questions.

Our desire is that many Christians would experience the joy and confidence in the Scriptures that is found throughout Psalm 119 – "How sweet are your words to my taste, sweeter than honey to my mouth!"

II. All about Book by Book

a. What is Book by Book?

Book by Book is a Bible Study resource with accompanying DVD. It has been designed principally for use in small groups, but can also be used for personal study or larger group situations.

b. The structure of Book by Book

The Study Guide

The Study Guide provides the following features for each section of study:

- A Key Truth to focus on the most important truth in that section of the Bible Book.
- A Mind-Map diagram giving an overview of the study.
- An explanation of the Bible text, divided under suitable headings.
- Further Questions, to stimulate deeper thought and discussion.
- A week of suggested daily Bible readings to fill out and explore the themes from the study.
- A Bible Study, with detailed questions, designed to lead the individual or group deeper into the text.
- A Bible Study answers section at the back of the study guide, for extra help if need be.

The DVD

Key features provided on each DVD are as follows:

- There is a 15 minute discussion on the DVD linked to each section of the Study Guide Bible passage
- The on-screen host is Richard Bewes, with co-host Paul Blackham. A specially invited guest joins them in the Bible discussions.

c. Some tips on how to use Book by Book

The beauty of Book by Book is that it offers not only great Biblical depth, but also flexibility of approach to study. Whether you are preparing to lead a small group, or study alone you will find many options open to you.

And it doesn't matter if you are a new Christian or more experienced at leading Bible studies, Book by Book can be adapted to your situation. You don't need to be a specially trained leader.

Group study: preparing

Select your study (preferably in the order of the book!)

- Watch the DVD programmes
- Read the commentary
- Use the suggested Bible questions...
- ...or formulate your own questions (the mind maps and key truths are a great guide for question structure)

Group study: suggested session structure

We recommend you set aside about an hour for each study

- 5 minutes – read the relevant section of the Bible
- 15 minutes – Watch the DVD programme
- 30 minutes – work through the Bible study questions (either your own or the ones in the guide), allowing time for discussion
- 10 minutes – If the study got the group thinking about wider issues of life today, Then consider the Further Questions to stimulate a broader discussion
- Taking it further – Suggest that group members look at some of the Daily Readings to follow up on the theme of the study

Given the volume of material you may even choose to take two weeks per study – using the DVD to generate discussion for one week and the Bible Study questions for the next.

Bookby**Book**

Individual study

There is no set way to conduct personal study — here are some ideas:

- Select your study (preferably in the order of the book!)

- Read the Bible passage and related commentary.

- Try looking at the Mind-Map diagrams and seeing how the book has a structure.

- Take a look at the Key Truths and decide if they are the same conclusions you had reached when you read the book.

- Perhaps focus on the week of daily Bible reading to help you to explore the rest of the Bible's teaching on the themes of each section of study.

- Work through the Bible Questions. Don't worry if you get stuck, there is an 'answers' section at the back of the guide!

III. An introduction to Acts

The book of Acts is the second volume of Luke's research. Luke 1:3 is addressed to "most excellent Theophilus" and Acts 1:1 is addressed to the same "Theophilus".

The first volume was Luke's attempt at an "orderly account" of "the things that have been fulfilled among us, just as they were handed down to us by those who from the first were eye-witnesses and servants of the word." Luke claims to have carefully investigated all that happened and wrote his ordered acount to bring together the eye-witness accounts with the Hebrew Scriptures that prophesied all these things. Luke ends his gospel with the conclsion that the Scriptures were fulfilled just as they had predicted, according to the eye-witness accounts of those who saw what actually happened.

We can summarise Luke's method in his biography of Jesus as *comparing the eye-witness accounts with the ancient Scriptural predictions*.

In this way the truth of Jesus of Nazareth can be proved.

In Luke's second volume, he has a slightly different agenda. He tells us in Acts 1:1-2:

> In my former book, Theophilus, I wrote about all that Jesus *began* to do and to teach until the day he was taken up to heaven, after giving instructions through the Holy Spirit to the apostles he had chosen.

So, the first volume was an account of what Jesus *began* to do, and this second volume is what Jesus coninued to do *after* His ascension. Through His apostles and by His Holy Spirit, the Lord Jesus continued His work from His throne in heaven.

The apostles have a unique foundational place in that work, but the church today is also part of that ongong work of Jesus. However, the book of Acts is not a complete account of what Jesus continued to do through His apostles. The book of Acts focusses on the apostle Peter for the first 12 chapters and then for the following 16 chapters the focus of attention switches to the apostle Paul. What about all the other apostles? What did they do and where did they go? The book of Acts sets its camera angle looking west from

Jerusalem, following the spread of the gospel to the nations across the northern stretches of the Mediterranean sea.

Luke chose a narrow perspective, ignoring the spread of the gospel across North Africa or into the nations east of Jerusalem. What of the apostle Thomas travelling reluctantly into India or Thaddeus' mission to Odessa? Whether Luke knew about these continuing works of Jesus or not, we cannot say, but what we do know is that Luke was a travelling companion with the apostle Paul. Luke wrote about the spread of the gospel to the nations that he was himself involved in.

Perhaps there is another factor to consider. The apostle Paul became involved in an intense dispute about the place of foreigners or 'Gentiles' in the people of God. As we follow Paul we are caught up in the vital questions surrounding the impact of Jesus on the continuing life of the people of God in relation to the Law of Moses. We don't know how Thomas or Thaddeus or the others grappled with these issues, but we know that Paul found himself in a life or death struggle over the freedom of the nations of the world to be full members of the people of God through trusting Jesus.

In other words, the Holy Spirit selected the lives of Peter and Paul to be recorded in the Bible in order to present the vital issues of *global Christianity* to the church in every age.

As Luke shows us the spread of the Way of Jesus through Peter and Paul so we are shown the transition from a merely *regional* Israel to a truly *global* Israel; from the *training period* of the Law of Moses to the full maturity after the Law completed its work. Through Peter & Paul and their companions we learn how to plant churches, how to present the truth of Jesus, how to live out the Way of Jesus in a complex and unbelieving world.

So, if Luke is our guide to this snapshot of the apostolic church, what do we know about Luke?

Luke was a doctor, as Paul describes in Colossians 4:14. Luke was also very interested in the way that the Roman authorities viewed the expansion of the ancient people of God. Luke is always careful to show that any trouble is never caused by the followers of Jesus but by the disruptive people who oppose the Way of Jesus.

The Jews had been given the special freedom to worship their own God across the Roman empire. For this reason Luke wanted to demonstrate that the Way of Jesus is not a new religion but is the true continuation of the life of Israel.

In the book of Luke, Jesus was declared to be innocent three times by the legal authorities. In the book of Acts, Paul is also declared to be innocent three times by the legal authorities. Luke wants the Roman authorities to see that there is nothing illegal about the followers of the Way.

Throughout Acts we also see public officials supporting and helping the apostles. In this way we see, as John Stott explains, that Luke is a diplomat for the Christian faith.[1]

In his biography of Jesus we see Luke's historical care and he exercised the same care in this second volume. Throughout the book Luke has an intimate and accurate knowledge of the civic life of the Roman empire.

> The historical framework is exact. In terms of time and place the details are precise and correct. One walks the steets and marketplaces, the theatres and assemblies of first-century Ephesus or Thessalonica, Corinth or Philippi, with the author of Acts. The great men of the cities, the magistrates, the mob and mob-leader are all there... It is similar with the narrative of Paul's judicial experiences before the tribunals of Gallio, Felix and Festus. As documents these narratives belong to the same historical series as the record of provincial and imperial trials in epigraphical and literary sources of the first and early second centuries AD.[2]

Furthermore, Luke doesn't merely record reliable eye-witness accounts. He also orders these accounts in line with the ancient Scriptures that predicted and explained these things in advance. Luke wants us to see that what happened was the *fulfilment* of Scripture, as seen by reliable eye-witnesses.

In this connection, Luke is a Biblical scholar. Lukes takes the time to record the Biblical exegesis of the apostles and incorporates his own appreciation of the Biblical background to the actions and events he records.

---

1   John Stott, *The Message of Acts*, IVP, Leicester, 1990, pages 25-29
2   A. N. Sherwin-White, quoted in Stott, page 25

Luke wants us to understand the theological significance of what we are reading. These are not meaningless happenings but the "globalisation of Israel". All the Gentile nations of the world had lived in a terrible spiritual darkness, alienated from the life of God for countless centuries.[3] The Cross of Jesus and the outpouring of the Spirit on all flesh meant that "citizenship in Israel" was being made available to all the nations of the world as the universal reality of Jesus went out to all the nations.

If Luke was a Gentile, then it makes sense that he had such a passion for explaining that the Way of Jesus was for every human being, whether Jew or Gentile.

Luke also shows us the spontaneous generosity and social care of the community of Jesus. *The Way of Jesus is not just a message for a hidden or future spiritual world, but is the Way to live right now, the answer to the needs of the world right here and now as well as in eternity.*

Luke was no mere academic collecting historical notes in his university study. He was one of Paul's co-workers, caught up in the thick of the action in the book of Acts. Luke was actually travelling with Paul when he was caught in the storm and shipwreck on his way to Rome. Several times we find the pronoun 'we' in the narrative, showing that Luke was certainly present at those times.

We find the 'we' pronoun at the following points: 16:10-17; 20:5-15; 21:1-18; 27:1-28:16. For this reason, we find an amazing level of historical detail and lengthy reports of key speeches. Luke's personal involvement adds such depth and colour to the book of Acts.

We also ought to be thankful to Luke for the way in which he introduces us to the character who is Paul. Without Luke's biographical detail, we would know so little about the man who wrote so many of the letters in the New Testament. Thanks to Luke however, we are able to know the man behind these letters and such knowledge adds weight to our reading of Paul's letters.

---

3   See Ephesians 2:12 – "remember that at that time you were separate from Christ, excluded from citizenship in Israel and foreigners to the covenants of the promise, without hope and without God in the world."

From his careful attention to cultural details to his constant attention to the role of women in the events, Luke gives us a rich picture of the human story. His concern for theology never overwhelms his concern for humanity. Rather, in the Way of Jesus Luke wants us to know that true human life is revealed. The Way of Jesus is the way of dignity, respect, compassion, generosity and justice. Human life can flourish in every facet only as we are saved from ourselves in Jesus.

The Studies

> **Key Truth**
>
> The apostles were appointed by Jesus to be faithful
> eye-witnesses to the whole world of all that He had done
> and said.

| a. Introducing volume 2 (1:1) | c. The choosing of Matthias (1:12-26) |

| b. The Ascension of Jesus (1:2-11) |

a. Introducing volume 2 (1:1)

Luke addresses the book to "Theophilus" – "God lover". It is quite possible that the whole two volume work is addressed to anybody who loves God or anyone who is seeking for God.

At the beginning of the gospel of Luke, he had referred to him as "most excellent Theophilus", which perhaps gives us a clue to his identity. In Acts 24:3 Paul speaks to "most excellent Felix" and in Acts 26:25 he addresses "most excellent Festus". Both of these men were civic governors, so it is reasonable to suppose that Luke wrote this mighty two volume work to a high-placed Roman politician as an 'apology' for the Way of Jesus of Nazareth. This would certainly fit with Luke's diplomatic purposes that we have referred to in the introduction.

Some have wondered whether Theophilus lived in Rome, given the way that the book ends. Others have suggested that "God-lover" may not be his real name but a way of referring to the character of this possibly new believer.

The book of Acts is the key background and explanation for the letters of the New Testament. Acts enables us to understand the specific circumstances that each of the churches were facing. Matthew Henry, the 18th century Bible scholar, refers to Acts as the book that "unites the Gospels to the Epistles".

b. The Ascension of Jesus (1:2-11)

The ascension of Jesus is the door out of the gospel of Luke and the door into this book of the continuing acts of Jesus. From His place of glory and authority at the throne of all creation, Jesus is able to resource, commission and direct His Body on earth in every age, in every place.

Some have wondered how Jesus spent those 40 days between "Easter" and Pentecost. What did He do? Where did He go? What did He teach? Who did He meet? Luke told us something about this at the end of his gospel when he showed us how Jesus took His disciples through the Hebrew Scriptures. Here at the beginning of Acts we learn some more:

Verse 2 – He gave instructions through the Holy Spirit to the apostles. This might seem strange because why would Jesus give instructions *through the Holy Spirit* when Jesus was still physically with them. It is very possible that He was teaching them how to receive and understand the instructions of the Holy Spirit while He was still with them. These apostles, like the ancient prophets, were the foundational teachers of the next age of Israel and they needed special training from Jesus for the coming years. It ought also to be born in mind that this is the way Jesus normally taught his disciples, as Luke has made clear in Luke 4:14-21.

Verse 3 – "After His suffering, He showed Himself to these men and gave many convincing proofs that He was alive. He appeared to them over a period of forty days and spoke about the kingdom of God." There are two key elements here: He made sure they could be faithful eye-witnesses of the physical, factual reality of His bodily resurrection; He gave them even more instruction concerning the kingdom of God. This teaching is included in what we hear from the apostles in the sermons and letters in the rest of the New Testament.[4]

It is very important to realise the importance of the eye-witness testimonies recorded for us in the Bible. The ancient Scriptures predicted that the

---

4   Some false teachers in the 2nd century AD spread the rumour that Jesus had 'secret teachings' (Gnosis) that He gave to His apostles during these 40 days. The church leaders of that time had to explain that the Scriptures were their authority and if the apostles had secret additional teachings, how come none of them knew about them when they had been converted either by the apostles themselves or by the next generation of followers of the apostles?

Promised Messiah would be physically raised from the dead, so it is vitally important that we know that those Scriptures were historically fulfilled in Jesus of Nazareth.

The final thing that we are told about Jesus' activities during this time is that He told the disciples to wait in Jerusalem for a baptism of the Holy Spirit – verse 4-5.

> "Do not leave Jerusalem, but wait for the gift my Father promised, which you have heard me speak about. For John baptised with water, but in a few days you will be baptised with the Holy Spirit."

The "gift my Father promised" was something that the disciples had heard Jesus speaking about and it is to be understood as the living reality that John's water baptism was a physical picture of. In Luke's gospel Jesus mentioned that the Holy Spirit would be given to those who ask for Him (Luke 11:13), but here Jesus specifically recalls the words of John the Baptist (Luke 3:14-17).

However, if we are looking for a specific promise from God the Father, as Jesus mentioned in Luke 24:49, then we are led back to the ancient prophet Joel – Joel 2:27-32. Before promising that anyone who calls on the Name of Jesus will be saved[5], the Father promises that there will be a day when He will pour out His Spirit on "all flesh", on people from every nation whether Jew or Gentile.

> "I will pour out my Spirit on all people. Your sons and daughters will prophesy, your old men will dream dreams, your young men will see visions. Even on my servants, both men and women, I will pour out my Spirit in those days."

Jesus states that this pouring out of the Spirit will be a "baptism" of the Spirit – verse 5. There are many words used in the Bible to describe the presence of the Spirit in a person – baptism, filling, coming upon, anointing etc. Some people see technical and subtle differences between each different word, but that is not the way the words are used. For example, note the simple words used by Peter to refer back to Pentecost in Acts 11:15, indicating that Cornelius experienced the same thing.

---

5   See Romans 10:14 and 1 Corinthians 1:2

The great reality here is that the Spirit who is eternally with the Father and the Son, the One who knows the deepest things of the life of the Father and Son (1 Corinthians 2:10-12), the One who gives life to all creatures throughout the world (Psalm 104:30), the One who empowers the Eternal Son to accomplish the glorious will of the Father (Luke 4:14-21), will also live with those who follow Jesus! He will reveal the deep things to us, give us His wonderful life and joy, and empower us to accomplish whatever Jesus wants us to do.

Is the baptism of the Spirit something that happens just once? Does this happen once at the beginning of the Christian's life in Jesus or is it a second stage of Christian life that people receive some time after following Jesus? We ask these questions only because there has been so much debate and division over these matters especially in modern times.

First, it is clear that nobody can be a follower of Jesus unless they have received the Spirit. Paul makes this point in Romans 8:9 and in John 3 Jesus describes how the Spirit brings the new birth that is given to all those who trust in Jesus. Nobody can genuinely confess in action that Jesus is the LORD God unless the Spirit lives within them (1 Corinthians 12:3). The prophecy of Joel specified that the Spirit will be poured out on everybody who calls on the Name of Jesus.

To imagine that a person could be a genuine follower of Jesus without receiving the Spirit is as strange as it is illogical. The confusion about this seems to arise from a misunderstanding about what happens to the Ephesian followers of John the Baptist in Acts 19 (which we will examine in detail when we get to that chapter).

Second, there is no reason to imagine that the baptism/filling of the Spirit is something that happened just once in the life of a follower of Jesus, in fact the very opposite seems to be true. Yes, we receive the Spirit when we begin to follow Jesus, yet we daily seek to be filled with the Spirit and there may be many times in our life when we experience the special filling of the Spirit to equip us for His service. We will see within the book of Acts that the same kind of experiences of the Spirit that the apostles received on the original Day of Pentecost happened many other times in their life and work. Note how Peter is repetitively filled with the Spirit each time he gets up to preach.

(Peter is filled with or baptised by the Holy Spirit three times in the first four chapters, 2:4, 4:8, 4:31.)

If we understand the Hebrew Scripture background to the word 'baptism' we realise that a "baptism of the Spirit" or "filling of the Spirit" can happen many times as the Spirit decides. 'Baptism' was one of the Greek words used to describe the ritual washings of the Law of Moses.[6] We see it used in Mark 7:1-4 concerning the daily ceremonial washings that the Pharisees were concerned about. These ceremonial washings were ways of preparing something for use, whether sacred or common. In the same way, although the Holy Spirit is always with the follower of Jesus, yet there can be times when He gives us extra joy or strength or gifts to handle the challenges that He is guiding us to face. If we want to know more of the Spirit, then we need to be out on the front-line of service, laying down our lives in service to others in the Name of Jesus. In this way the Spirit will keep supplying us with all we need, renewing our strength and sharing His overflowing joy.

So, the fact that the disciples were to wait for the empowering presence of the Spirit, does not mean that they did not have the Spirit with them. They knew the presence of the Spirit with them as followers of Jesus. They had already been born again by the power of the Spirit.[7] He had equipped them on the missions they had already done within Israel. When the disciples were anxious about Jesus' departure, He said "And I will ask the Father, and He will give you another Counsellor to be with you for ever – the Spirit of truth. The world cannot accept Him, because it neither sees Him nor knows Him. But you know Him, for He lives with you and will be in you."[8] The Spirit has been with them and will continue to be in them when Jesus is no longer physically with them.

---

6   In the Greek translation of the Hebrew Scriptures carried out in 300BC (the Septuagint), the Greek word *baptidzo* is often used for these ceremonial washings in Exodus and Leviticus.

7   Note Ezekiel 18:30-32 when the LORD God offered new birth to the people many hundreds of years before Acts 2.

8   Even this verse is taken in strange directions! There are those who see a vast difference between "He lives with you" and "He will be in you". They have argued that the Spirit was only with the disciples before Pentecost, but after that day the Spirit was in them! It is very unlikely that such a huge doctrinal pronouncement would hang on such a tiny difference in preposition! The context is vital. Jesus is telling the disciples that they don't need to fear the fact that He is returning to the Father because the same Spirit who is with them will remain in them even when He has gone.

The disciples didn't ask any questions about the baptism of the Spirit, but they did want to press Jesus on the future – "Lord, are you at this time going to restore the kingdom to Israel?" (verse 6).

There are three parts to this question. First they wanted to know if the fulfilment of the Kingdom of God was going to happen "at this time". They were interested in knowing when history would reach its conclusion, as so many disciples have been down the ages. Second, they are thinking of the power and glory of a kingdom like that of earthly kingdoms. In that sense they are looking backwards rather than forwards. Third, they were focussed on the geographical region of Israel rather than the global community of all the nations.

Jesus answers the question in a way that confronts each part of the question. First, the specific date of the Day of Justice is in the hands of the Father alone. Jesus the Eternal Son doesn't even know that date![9] Just as Jesus is content to trust in the will of the Father, so must we. We must stay away from the unhelpful and unbiblical speculations that try to predict the Day of Justice. Second, the disciples wanted to become rulers in Jesus kingdom (Matthew 20:21; Mark 10:37) and Jesus had to tell them that their future involved serious service as witnesses of Jesus. Their future was not one of ease and comfort, but suffering and faithful service. They were on the path to glory, but they had to follow Jesus as faithful witnesses. Third, Jesus vision is not for the geographical region of Israel alone. He goes back to the original vision given to Abraham in Genesis 12:2-3. The kingdom of Jesus is not a regional power like the kingdoms of this earth. It isn't defined by genetics and nationality like other kingdoms. The kingdom of Jesus is for the whole world, all the nations of the world.

From being fairly small-minded Jewish tradesmen, these disciples were sent out into a vast world of varied cultures, languages and nationalities. Jesus words made these disciples into global revolutionaries.

The same vision needs to strike us with the same force. So often our tendency is to become fixed in our local ways, to settle into the divisions of this passing age. We need to follow Jesus into His global revolution, and that will rarely fit in with the comfortable ways and assumptions that may be natural to us.

---

9   Matthew 24:36 – "No-one knows about that day or hour, not even the angels in heaven, nor the Son, but only the Father."

Having set the vision of His global kingdom before the disciples, Jesus "was taken up before their very eyes and a cloud hid Him from their sight."

It is hard for us to imagine what actually happened here. Nothing like this had ever happened before and it has never happened since! The closest parallel might be the time when Elijah was carried up to heaven in a fiery chariot (2 Kings 2:11) and that sounds very strange. Jesus was not just floating up into the rain clouds at the edge of the earth's atmosphere. Nor was Jesus shooting around the solar system like some kind of science fiction character. No, Jesus was going beyond the first heaven (the atmosphere) and the second heaven (the universe of galaxies) into the third heaven (the place where the Father has established His throne, where millions of angels gather). When we consider the vast difference in glory between the first and second heavens, we cannot imagine the infinite majesty of the third heaven. How did Jesus travel to that Majestic Glory? As the clouds of glory enveloped Him, how did His ascension happen?

It is very unwise for us to impose the language of science fiction ("going into a parallel dimension", "journeying to an alternate universe"), because the reality is very likely to be something so utterly different than the tiny conceptions we deal in. It is true Jesus left this place, but he hasn't gone too far away because in Acts 7:55, Stephen sees him.

What we do need to remember is that Jesus was exalted to the highest place in the whole creation. He has been given a seat next to the Father in the throneroom of the universe. The glory and authority that belongs to Him is formally and officially confirmed and declared in His glorious ascension. The work of atonement that He had accomplished on earth, His own blood that He had shed in death, was taken up into the Most Holy Place where the whole of creation could be changed and redeemed.

The disciples were stunned by what they saw and were left standing with their mouths open. Two helpful angels were available to help them deal with the situation. Yes, the ascension of Jesus was amazing, but one day He would return from heaven with just the same glory. Jesus is a citizen of planet earth. His passport belongs to this world and He is a member of the human race. He has travelled away from home for a time, but He will certainly return. On the Day of Justice the Highest heaven will follow Jesus down to the earth forever more.

c. The choosing of Matthias (1:12-26)

In stunned wonder the disciples all gathered together in Jerusalem. Luke tells us that there were about 120 of them including the women who had sponsored Jesus. In addition His natural family were part of the group with Mary and presumably Jude and James. In those initial days what was the distinguishing mark of this group of Jesus followers? Verse 14 — "They all joined together constantly in prayer…" We can always tell the true spiritual health of any church by visiting the prayer meeting/prayer times. Typically less than 20% of any church actually bothers to pray together. The 20% who pray together are usually the 20% who actually do all the work.

Peter remembered that ancient David, 1000 years before, had prophesied the very situation they were in. In Psalm 69:25 David speaks of the fate that belongs to the wicked who oppose the Divine Messiah[10], but Psalm 109 is even more intense. The Messiah speaks of how He is betrayed by those close to Him, by those He has invited to be His friends. Therefore, the evil man who betrayed Him will suffer all the consequences of sin, all the curses of rejecting the LORD God, including his place of leadership being taken by somebody else (Psalm 109:8).

The terrible fate of Judas was not only important to the original biographers of Jesus, but also the wider church in those days. Matthew was concerned to show that Judas died the cursed death of Deuteronomy 21:22-23, so he gives the briefest account noting simply that Judas hanged himself. Luke gives more detail, noting that Judas heavy body fell from the hanging and burst open on the field he had bought. Early writers go even further, explaining how grossly fat Judas became before the hanging, falling and bursting.[11]

On the basis of the Psalms, Peter felt that they needed to take immediate action to replace Judas. Knowing the significance of the number 12 through the Scriptures, it was obvious that there had to be 12 apostles, but who was to fill the vacant position?

---

10   Note especially Psalm 69:21 as a further sign that the Psalm was written about Jesus rather than David Himself. (Compare John 19:28-30).

11   In the *Fragments of Papias* we read "Judas walked about in this world a sad example of impiety; for his body having swollen to such an extent that he could not pass where a chariot could pass easily, he was crushed by the chariot, so that his bowels gushed out."

The job description is important – "it is necessary to choose one of the men who have been with us the whole time the Lord Jesus went in and out among us, beginning from John's baptism to the time when Jesus was taken up from us. For one of these must become a witness with us of his resurrection."

An apostle had to be a person who had been an eye-witness of all that had happened during the life and ministry of Jesus. The apostles had to be eye-witnesses of what had happened – just as Luke had emphasised at the beginning of his biography of Jesus (Luke 1:2). This definition of apostle could not really apply to church leaders in any other generation.

So eager were the Eleven to find a replacement, that they quickly lined up two candidates – Joseph and Matthias. These two had been part of the group for the past three years, since Jesus had been baptised by John, and we can be sure they were excellent candidates.

However, was this the right thing to do? Was it not possible that the LORD Jesus had thought about the replacement for Judas Himself and had already got a candidate in mind, somebody who would fill the position very well and add a vital ingredient to the passion and direction of their global mission in those early years? Luke certainly will present us with someone who is also an apostle, someone who becomes an equal of the original Eleven, someone who even Peter acknowledges as a writer of Scriptures (2 Peter 3:15-16). In all fairness, we don't hear anything more of Matthias, yet we hear lots more of the other apostle that the LORD Jesus appointed Himself – Paul of Tarsus.

The problem may lie in the way that they put the matter to the LORD in Acts 2:24-26. In the Hebrew Scriptures decisions seem to have been made with the Urim and Thummim. We do not really know how these were used, but it is said that these two stones each had a dark side and a light side. If the stones were both on the light side then it meant "yes". If the stones were both on the dark side then it meant "no", but if they were different then it meant something like "neither". Whatever the case of how the Urim and Thummim were used, yet there obviously needed to be a way for the Lord God to choose neither of the options that mere human beings put to Him.

In Acts 2:24 they ask "which of these two is your choice Lord?", whereas the Lord may not want either man. They cast lots, and it is true that the decision of the lot lies with the Lord, yet what if neither option was the Lord's choice?

It is very reassuring to know that these apostles could make mistakes and still be useful to the Lord. This group of 120 would totally change the history of the world in Jesus' Name, yet the very first decision they made was mistaken! We all need to be encouraged that even when we make mistakes and let the Lord down, yet He will still use us if we keep following Him. He is always ready to give us another chance.

Throughout the second half of the book of Acts we seem to get the real decision of the Lord concerning Judas' replacement.

Study 1   Bible Questions [12]

Acts 1:1-11

1. Verse 1 – Read Luke 1:1-4. What are the similarities between Luke's first book and his second one? What are the differences?

2. Verses 2-3 – Why was Jesus not taken up into heaven straight after his resurrection? What did he do before he was taken up and why? What do these forty days tell us about our future? (See also Philippians 3:21.)

3. Verses 4-5 – Why did Jesus want the apostles to wait in Jerusalem to receive the Holy Spirit? Who sends the Holy Spirit?

4. Verse 6 – What does the apostle's question reveal about their priorities and aspirations? Is their question a reasonable one? Why?

5. Verses 7-8 – How does Jesus counter their views and what does he tell them they must do? What sort of a job would this be? What help would they need and have?

6. Verse 9 – Why did Jesus have to be taken from their sight? Why was it important that Jesus was taken up "before their very eyes" instead of just disappearing one day?

7. Verses 10-11 – In what way was the question of the angels unreasonable? How did they encourage the apostles?

8. Verses 1-11 – How are our circumstances similar to the circumstances the apostles were in when Jesus left? How are they different? What command has Jesus given each of us? What help has he given each of us?

---

12   I must pay tribute to the great effort and faithful labour of Richard Koelling in working on the Bible studies, further questions and Bible readings. In addition to all that, his comments throughout this study have been vitally important.

BookbyBook

What are some of the common misunderstandings about the future that are dispelled by Jesus' appearance to his followers for forty days after his resurrection? What is the significance of forty days?

Why was Jesus taken "up" and not just taken away? What might this signify? What do clouds seem to signify in the Bible?

Were the disciples right to use the Bible in the way they did to chose a twelfth apostle? How might we use the Bible in the same way? Why did there need to be twelve apostles?

Study 1	Daily Readings
Day 1	Luke 24:1-35
Day 2	Luke 24:36-53
Day 3	Matthew 28
Day 4	Mark 16
Day 5	John 21
Day 6	Joel 2:18-32
Day 7	Psalm 68

The daily Bible readings are an opportunity to not only read through all of the material in the book under study, but also to read parts of the Bible that relate to the themes and issues that we have been considering. We try to make sure that we receive light from the whole Bible as we think through the key issues each week.

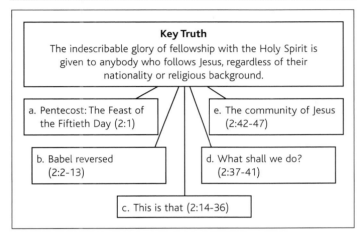

Study 2   "This is That" Acts 2

Key Truth
The indescribable glory of fellowship with the Holy Spirit is given to anybody who follows Jesus, regardless of their nationality or religious background.

a. Pentecost: The Feast of the Fiftieth Day (2:1)

b. Babel reversed (2:2-13)

c. This is that (2:14-36)

d. What shall we do? (2:37-41)

e. The community of Jesus (2:42-47)

a. Pentecost: The Feast of the Fiftieth Day (2:1)

The Feast of Pentecost[13] *(the Feast of the Fiftieth Day)* was the harvest festival of the ancient Jewish feasts, occurring 50 days after the feast of Firstfruits.[14]

The feast of Firstfruits happened when the very first crops were harvested. These first bits of the harvest were offered to the LORD to show that it is the LORD alone who causes the plants to grow, the animals to reproduce, the sun to shine, the rain to fall and the seasons to come and go. However, those first parts of the harvest only represented a sample of the full harvest that was to come later. At the Feast of Pentecost they would celebrate the full harvest that they had only sampled before.

The Festival was probably recalling the fact that it took 50 days for The Angel of the LORD[15] to lead the people from captivity in Egypt to meet with the Unseen LORD at Mount Sinai. Leaving Egypt was the first experience of

---

13   The word *Pentecost* comes from the Greek word meaning fiftieth.

14   See Leviticus 23:16-22; Numbers 28:26-31; Deuteronomy 16:9-12

15   The pre-incarnate Jesus.

redemption (the firstfruits of their new life) but the purpose of it all was to have fellowship with the Most High God. At Sinai they heard the voice of the Father and when the ram's horn sounded they were supposed to go up the mountain to meet with Him.[16]

The Feast of Pentecost was about receiving all that had been promised.

The Feast of the Fiftieth Day was full of expectation and hope. It was a day of great celebration, enjoying all the wonderful things that the LORD God had given to his people – Deuteronomy 16:10-12. In Leviticus 23:17 we are told that they would eat bread baked *with* yeast. They did this because unlike the time of Passover when they were remembering how they needed to be rescued from slavery, from a world falling under God's judgement, now in the Feast of Pentecost they were celebrating the fact that they had been redeemed into their own Promised Land, a land full of blessing, a land where there was plenty of time to wait for the dough to rise as they baked their bread![17]

In the same way, the presence of the Spirit with the Jewish people who trusted in the Promised Messiah had only ever been the first sample, the first fruits, of the full harvest. The full harvest is a Spirit-filled humanity of every people, race, culture and language. When we read Leviticus 23:22 the Feast of Pentecost was a time when the ancient church remembered to make provision for the poor and needy, whether they were Jew or Gentile. There was a longing in that ancient festival to share the blessings of the LORD God with everybody, of every nation.

Looked at from another angle we see how the Holy Spirit right now brings the harvest of the New Creation into our current experience and life. He allows people of every nation to experience the kind of life and joy and peace and fruitfulness that we will fully enjoy in the New Creation future. In the Spirit the New Creation is already among us, the harvest is already happening.

For all these reasons we can fully understand why it is at the Feast of Pentecost that the Holy Spirit is poured out for people of every nation, whether Jew or Gentile, whether near or far from the God of Abraham who has blessings for all nations.

---

16   For more on this see the Book by Book Exodus study guide.

17   Compare Exodus 12:39. Bread baked without yeast was always a reminder of the need for redemption, the need for rescue, the need to get out of the world and cling to the Living God who saves.

b. Babel reversed (2:2-13)

The 120 disciples were all gathered together when wind and fire came from heaven and the whole building was literally in danger of falling down.[18] This wind and fire are Biblical signs of the presence of the Living God, yet the wind and fire are not where the LORD is really known. It is when the disciples open their mouths to speak that the real presence of the Spirit is revealed.[19] He had given them the ability to speak in all the different languages of the world.

When Jesus had promised that His disciples would go out to all the nations of the world to share His kingdom, it must have seemed impossible. These simple fishermen were not cosmopolitan world-travellers. They did not have all the cross-cultural training that we might think is essential for any such undertaking. They hadn't learned the languages or learned all the key cultural symbols for the nations of the world. Yet, in an incredible miracle that has hardly ever been repeated in the history of the world, these followers of Jesus were turned into fluent orators in all the languages of the world.

When we try to recover what happened to all these disciples as they headed off to the different nations of the world we can make reasonable guesses as to which disciples were given which languages. It seems fairly likely that Thomas was given the relevant Indian languages, given that he ended up planting churches in South India. He may also have gone on into China. Peter was involved in Asia Minor (Turkey) and may have gone further, into Europe.

The key point is that the LORD Jesus had sent them out with a specific task to complete. Yes, it looked impossible, almost ridiculous, and yet the Almighty Eternal Spirit of the Living God was easily able to give them everything they needed to complete the task. When we look back into the Hebrew Scriptures and see the extraordinary charismatic gifts that the Spirit gave to Moses, Elijah, Bezalel, Oholiab, Daniel, David, Samson, Nehemiah, Esther, Joshua and all the others, then we can have boundless confidence that when we obediently serve Jesus we will always be equipped with all we need.

---

18 Compare Isaiah 6:1-4

19 Compare 1 Kings 19:1-18 when Elijah learned that although the earthquake, wind and fire showed the LORD's presence, yet it was in the calm words of the LORD that Elijah really found the Living God.

Up until this time the praises and prayers of the Living God had always been in the Hebrew language. The Jews scattered around the world, regardless of their original culture or language would have had to learn Hebrew in order to understand what was happening in the temple in Jerusalem.

We will see throughout the book of Acts that the fact that people were worshipping the Living God in 'foreign' or 'pagan' languages was quite shocking and revolutionary to the original Jewish followers of Jesus.

The multinational, multilingual Jewish crowds in Jerusalem were amazed at what was happening. They had never before heard the wonders of God proclaimed in their own native languages.

> Acts 2:7-11 "Are not all these men who are speaking Galileans? Then how is it that each of us hears them in his own native language? Parthians, Medes and Elamites; residents of Mesopotamia, Judea and Cappadocia, Pontus and Asia, Phrygia and Pamphylia, Egypt and the parts of Libya near Cyrene; visitors from Rome (both Jews and converts to Judaism); Cretans and Arabs — we hear them declaring the wonders of God in our own languages!"

Ever since the tower of Babel the different languages of the world had stood as a barrier between all the different nations of the world. Finding a common mind and a common understanding was impossible because of the confusion of languages that the LORD God had brought on humanity back in Genesis 11:9.[20] Humanity back then had tried to find a point of unity for all the people of the world, a project that would unify the world together. However, the LORD God would not allow a sinful and arrogant unity for humanity. There can be only one point of unity for the whole human race — Jesus the Glorious Mediator who can break down every barrier with His love and humility, with His death and resurrection.

---

20   It is unlikely that all the different languages were created by the LORD God at Babel. The variety of languages is not a curse, but a blessing. If we look back into Genesis 10 we see that there were many different languages before the tower of Babel. However, Genesis 11:1 tell us that the whole world had "one mind and a common understanding". In other words the difference in language and culture did not create a barrier to understanding. After the arrogance of Babel, the Lord God caused the confusion of languages so that now even people who speak the same language find it very hard to have one mind and a common understanding.

In many ways, then, Acts 2 stands as the answer to Genesis 11. The confusion of Babel is reversed in the communion of the Spirit. The tower of Babel is rejected and the Cross of Jesus is confirmed as the place where all the nations may meet together and find common understanding.

The great Bible scholar of the 18th century Matthew Henry describes the situation so well:

> "The Spirit, like fire, melts the heart, burns up the dross, and kindles pious and devout affections in the soul; in which, as in the fire on the altar, the spiritual sacrifices are offered up. They were all filled with the Holy Ghost, more than before. They were filled with the graces of the Spirit, and more than ever under his sanctifying influences; more weaned from this world, and better acquainted with the other. They were more filled with the comforts of the Spirit, rejoiced more than ever in the love of Christ and the hope of heaven: in it all their griefs and fears were swallowed up. They were filled with the gifts of the Holy Ghost; they had miraculous powers for the furtherance of the gospel."[21]

c. This is that (2:14-36)

Clearly some explanation was required. Alcohol does not grant people the gift of speaking in foreign languages, so Peter and the Eleven began to explain the situation to the crowd in all their different languages.

- How could men so early in the morning be so full of Spirit?
- How could they speak the wonders of God in the foreign, pagan languages of the world?
- How did this connect to the strange events that had occurred in Israel regarding Jesus of Nazareth?

Peter got to the key issue straight away. All these things had been predicted by the prophet Joel long ago. This was the day when the prophecy of Joel was actually being fulfilled.

---

21   This is from the abridged version of Matthew Henry's commentary.

What had Joel prophesied? The prophecy of Joel comes when the nation of Judah was facing terrible ruin. The LORD was bringing terrible armies against Judah and there would be little left after they had finished their destruction. Like locusts they would strip the land of everything. Yet, there was still time to repent and after the destruction there would be a day when the LORD God would deal with the nations. There would be salvation for the nations and they too would experience the power of the Spirit. Yet there would also be condemnation and judgement on the nations until the whole world was put right.

Peter isolates the prophecy concerning the salvation of the nations and proclaims that the very thing that Joel had spoken of was happening around them that very day. Young and old from every nation could receive the Spirit of the Living God. The very order of the cosmos was being turned around and shaken up (Acts 2:19-20). Yes, anyone from any nation who called on the Name of the Lord would be saved.

It sounds so incredible. To the original audience of Acts 2 it must have seemed blasphemous and impossible. For 1,500 years anybody who was going to be saved needed to first become a Jew and be carefully apprenticed into the Law of Moses, possibly over several generations (see Deuteronomy 23:7-8). How could all this be forgotten? How could people who had no idea of the ways and character of the LORD God of Israel be allowed into fellowship with Him?

How could pagans be acceptable to God unless they first became Jews?[22]

This is the fundamental question that Peter addresses right away by telling them about Jesus. Jesus was obviously the supreme Man of God, given His wonderful teaching, miracles and good deeds (verse 22). Yet, the Sovereign God purposed that His perfect Servant would be betrayed and rejected. He was put to death in the worst possible way, by being nailed to a tree (see Deuteronomy 21:22-23) to bring the curse of God against Him.

---

22 We get something of this today when Christians try to make people give up all their sins and vices *before* they are welcomed into the Christian family as fellow saints. Yet, the situation in Acts 2 would have seemed much more radical and shocking simply because it seemed to go against the whole Law of Moses.

All humanity, Jew and Gentile alike, stood shoulder to shoulder against the divinely approved Messiah. Any distinction between saints and pagans, Jews and Gentiles, natives and foreigners, was wiped out when that happened.

Yet, the Living God sided with Jesus and raised Him from the dead, putting Jesus right back into the middle of the picture. How could death keep hold of the One who invented life?!

David was a prophet and wrote about Jesus. In particular David wrote about the resurrection of Jesus in Psalm 16, predicting that the Messiah would not only be killed but would also be raised from the dead before His body had a chance to decay.

David obviously wasn't talking about himself because he did die and his body did rot away.

Now, Peter and the others were eye-witnesses of the fact that God's Messiah who had been rejected by both Jews and Gentiles was not only brought back to life but has been installed as the King of the Universe.

This is very serious. If you find yourselves in opposition to the Master of the Universe, the Omnipotent Ruler of the universe, then you are in serious trouble. Psalm 110 said that from that lofty position all His enemies would be dealt with.

However, if all humanity, Jew and Gentile alike, are lumped together in this doomed mess and condemnation, then they are also lumped together in the wonderful twist in the story. Exalted to the highest place, Jesus is not using His power to destroy everybody but to fulfil the most ancient prophecies in the Scriptures. He is offering salvation to anybody in the world, Jew or Gentile, who will call out to Him asking for mercy.

The Holy Spirit, who was previously reserved only for Jewish insiders, would now have fellowship with anybody from any nation or religion that follows Jesus.

Peter's explanation was powerful. He showed how Jesus had been prophesied for long ages and how the Jewish nation had ended up alongside the Gentiles in opposition to the LORD God. Yet, Peter had also indicated that there was wonderful good news in all this. Jesus is the long predicted Messiah who had come not to destroy the world but to bring salvation and divine fellowship to everybody in the world.

d. What shall we do? (2:37-41)

With Peter's heart and mind full of the Spirit and the ears of the crowd opened by the Spirit it is no surprise that his words struck into the very deepest places – verse 37. They wanted to know what to do. They could not afford to be on the wrong side of Jesus and they desperately wanted to become involved with the wonderful global salvation that was starting right under their very noses.

Peter's reply was direct but packed with truth: "Repent and be baptised, every one of you, in the name of Jesus Christ for the forgiveness of your sins. And you will receive the gift of the Holy Spirit. The promise is for you and your children and for all who are far off – for all whom the Lord our God will call."

The first thing they had to do was change their mind, turn around and start following Jesus. Repentance is not so much about feeling sorry or tearful (though that is often part of it) but everything to do with the commitments of our heart and the actions that follow. Repentance means turning away from the way we have been living and the things we have trusted and turning to Jesus, trusting Him and showing that trust by doing everything that He has commanded.

Secondly, they had to be baptised. This was familiar territory to this crowd. Many of them may have been involved in the baptism of the nation that John the Baptist had done, yet more fundamentally they were used to all the ceremonial washings of the Law of Moses. When a priest was set aside for serving the LORD, they would be baptised (ceremonially washed). This baptism not only cleansed them but also showed their identity with the people they represented. When a sacrificed animal was being prepared for the altar, it was baptised so that it was acceptable to the LORD. Whenever Jewish people had become unclean they had to be baptised in order to be restored. When Peter told them that they needed to be baptised with their repentance, that would all be quite normal for these Jewish enquirers.

However, the new element was that their baptism was to be in the Name of Jesus the Messiah and would bring the forgiveness of their sins. For a Jew, forgiveness of sins was all about substitution. If an animal was sacrificed at the temple as a substitute for the sinner, then there could be forgiveness of sin.

Peter told them that if they washed in the Name of Jesus, showing their identification with Jesus, then He was their substitute. Jesus' death is sufficient to deal with all sin and no more animal sacrifices were required.

The Jewish system of animal sacrifice was no longer needed and anybody and everybody could receive forgiveness of sin through the death of Jesus. Furthermore, the proof of the efficacy of Jesus' death was this: anybody who repented and was baptised in His name would receive the outpoured Holy Spirit, regardless of their background, nationality or religion. Yes, this was not only for the Jews and their children, but also for those who were very far from the Living God – verse 39.

The world had set itself against Jesus, the LORD God of Israel. He was exalted to the highest place and would soon judge the world. While there is still time we all need to escape "this corrupt generation" and find terms of peace and fellowship on the basis of Jesus' death.

It is fascinating to note that 3,000 people began to follow Jesus on that day. Way back at the original 50th day when the people were gathered around Mount Sinai, 3,000 people had been killed when they turned away from the LORD God – Exodus 32:28.

e.   The community of Jesus (2:42-47)

Were the words of Peter true?

Could it really be true that anybody and everybody can receive forgiveness and be welcomed into the Divine Life by following Jesus?

The truth of it all was demonstrated in the kind of community that was formed by those people who responded to the apostle's teaching. This first example of the global community of Jesus was hungry to learn of the ways of Jesus from the apostles. They were united together, praying together and eating the thanksgiving meal together in order to remember the death of Jesus that saved them.

Yet, this was not about pious sentiments. The world has seen enough of 'religious communities' that talk a good talk but never really do anything. Here was something genuinely different.

All the believers were together and had everything in common. Selling their possessions and goods, they gave to anyone as he had need.

We can always tell if people are serious about their commitments if we keep our eye on their diary and their wallet. Anyone can speak pious platitudes but how does it affect our diaries and our wallets. The diaries and wallets of these Jesus-followers had been so profoundly affected that... they had probably sold them! There was such a profound desire for the overflowing generous life of the Father, Son and Spirit to be expressed among them, that they could not bear to see anyone in need. How could they cling onto earthly possessions when the love of Jesus within them yearned to give all they could to help others?

Whenever the followers of Jesus behave like this the world (and often the 'church' too!) becomes very threatened! This kind of behaviour turns the world upside down. It is the true revolution of Jesus, living just as He lived.

Yes, they didn't all immediately sell absolutely everything they owned, but sold as the need arose. They still met together in their homes, yet everything was shared.

May we never be so worried by extreme examples of this that we never get anywhere close to it! Lord Jesus, please set us free to live Acts 2:42-45 right now in our day and age. Lord Jesus, set us free from the tyranny of our possessions, from the love of money, from the need for security in this world, from selfishness and greed. Lord Jesus, may we genuinely love each other as you and the Father and the Spirit are united in love. Lord Jesus, may we see those in need as our own flesh and blood so that we give them all we can. Lord Jesus, have mercy on us.

With such a glorious faithfulness to the Way of Jesus it is no surprise that daily people were joining them. It is just as Jesus said: "You are the light of the world. A city on a hill cannot be hidden. Neither do people light a lamp and put it under a bowl. Instead they put it on its stand, and it gives light to everyone in the house. In the same way, let your light shine before men, that they may see your good deeds and praise your Father in heaven." (Matthew 5:14-16)

Study 2   Bible Questions

Acts 2:1-13

1. Verse 1 – What is the significance of the Day of Pentecost? What did it signify for a believing Jew? Why then was this the right day for the Holy Spirit to be poured out in this way? See also Leviticus 23:15-22.

2. Verse 2 – Why was there a sound like a violent wind from heaven at this time and what might the apostles have thought of this?

3. Verse 3 – What is the significance of these "tongues of fire" separating and then resting on each person individually? Why is the Holy Spirit represented as fire?

4. Verse 4 – What was the immediate effect of this experience on the believers?

5. Verse 5 – Who were the people staying in Jerusalem at this time and where were they all from? Why is this significant?

6. Verse 6-8 – What amazed the listening crowds most about this event?

7. Verses 9-11 – What role do the Egyptians, the Medes and Mesopotamia play in the life of God's people throughout the Bible? What does this say about the destination of this new life?

8. Verse 13 – Why would some mock this event? On which other significant occasions do some people mock and seem to miss the point?

9. Verses 1-13 – What do all these strange events on this important day mean for the apostles and what do they mean for us? How necessary is the gift of tongues in our churches? Why?

Study 2   Further Questions

In Acts 1:5, Jesus told his disciples that they would soon be "baptised" with the Holy Spirit. Yet when the event occurs, they are described as being "filled with the Holy Spirit" (Acts 2:4). What does this use of different terms mean?

What is the primary reason for the giving of the gift of languages or tongues? What would have been the effect of this gift on the Day of Pentecost if there had been no one who spoke a foreign language present? Read 1 Corinthians 14. How does that fit with the way the gift of languages is referred to in Acts 2? What examples are there of this gift on the Old Testament?

Where did the new international church celebrate communion and how did they view this sacrament? How is our understanding of the breaking of bread different to theirs? Why?

Study 2   Daily Readings

Day 1	Acts 2:14-47
Day 2	Leviticus 23:15-22
Day 3	Deuteronomy 16:9-12
Day 4	Genesis 11:1-9
Day 5	1 Corinthians 14:1-25
Day 6	Psalm 16
Day 7	Revelation 7:9-17

The daily Bible readings are an opportunity to not only read through all of the material in the book under study, but also to read parts of the Bible that relate to the themes and issues that we have been considering. We try to make sure that we receive light from the whole Bible as we think through the key issues each week.

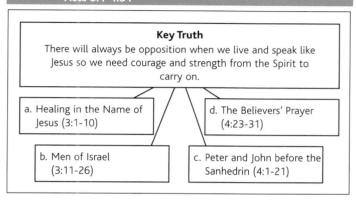

Study 3 "Enable your servants to speak your words"
Acts 3:1-4:31

Key Truth
There will always be opposition when we live and speak like Jesus so we need courage and strength from the Spirit to carry on.

a. Healing in the Name of Jesus (3:1-10)

d. The Believers' Prayer (4:23-31)

b. Men of Israel (3:11-26)

c. Peter and John before the Sanhedrin (4:1-21)

a. Healing in the Name of Jesus (3:1-10)

It all seemed too wonderful. Jesus of Nazareth, the Divine Man, lived the perfect life and welcomes everybody to join Him in living the life of God. Three thousand people did join the Jesus revolution and lived the extraordinary life of Jesus of generosity, love, truth and faithfulness.

What could possibly go wrong!? How could anybody resist such a compelling life and truth and way?

Luke is not interested in writing mere propaganda. He wanted to show his readers what it is really like to be a faithful follower of Jesus – both the joys and the sorrows.

The formal division between 'church' and 'temple' had not yet happened, so the Jesus followers continued to participate in the prayer and worship at the temple each day. The hope must have been that the whole of Israel would fulfil her destiny, recognise her Messiah and join the global expansion of Israel.

As Peter and John were going for afternoon prayers at the temple, they saw a congenitally lame man. Each day, for 40 years (see 4:22) this man was carried to the temple gate where people could provide for him as they went to worship. He asked the apostles for money, but then instead of just ignoring the beggar (as most of us would do), Peter looked directly at him. How many people had really looked at this man? Who valued him enough to genuinely connect with him as a fellow human being?

Peter told the man to return the look. The man had obviously been begging in an absent-minded way, because it is only at this point that he gives Peter and John his attention – verse 5.

We have seen the life and teaching of Jesus in this apostolic community, but now Luke shows us that the same miraculous power of the Spirit was also among them. It was as if Jesus were still on the earth! Peter and John commanded the man to walk in the Name of Jesus... and just as when Jesus had healed people, some incredible strengthening growth happened within the man's feet and ankle's. Perhaps his feet had not been formed properly, but this man had never used his ankles or feet! Suddenly he had the feet and ankles that he always dreamed of... with the muscle and co-ordination to use them! Anyone who has been incapacitated for a long time knows how they have to re-learn the ability to walk. However, this man was not only given the bone and muscle to walk and jump and dance, but his brain was wired with all the right instincts and commands![23]

Sharing money had already made a difference in the community (2:42-45), but some people needed a lot more than money. The apostles, as the appointed representatives of Jesus, were empowered to bring this miraculous healing in the Name of Jesus of Nazareth. Now this healed man used his renewed body to go into the temple to worship the Living God who had done this for him.

This was sure to get attention. Having been placed at the temple gate every day for years and years, it was certain that everybody had seen him. Now here he was, jumping around and shouting out praise to the LORD God. If the community of Jesus had already made a stir, now they had created a riot!

---

23 Having had a very serious accident when I was a child I remember how difficult it was to re-learn how to walk. I am always amazed that this man who had been born without proper feet and ankles was immediately able to walk and jump.

b. Men of Israel (3:11-26)

Luke notes that the crowds gathered at Solomon's colonnade, perhaps indicating that true wisdom was about to be given to the people. Peter diverts attention away from them and instead explains the identity of Jesus.

The God of Abraham, Isaac and Jacob will never give His glory to another (Isaiah 42:8), yet He has glorified His servant Jesus. However, even though Jesus shares the divine glory, the people of Jerusalem rejected Him and handed Him over to be killed. They chose an evil man rather than the Holy One of Israel – verse 14.[24] In a ghastly, impossible paradox they killed the Author of Life – verse 15.

Nevertheless, the Living God raised Jesus from the dead and the apostles had seen this resurrected Holy One with their own eyes. The fact that they had healed the man in the Name of Jesus was proof that Jesus was not only alive but that He is the Lord. Jesus can be completely trusted for everything in life and death – verse 16.

This should be very worrying for the people of Jerusalem. Killing the Divine Author of Life is surely the worst possible offence. Yet, behind their betrayal and evil a deeper, divine purpose was at work.

The ancient Scriptures always predicted that the Messiah would suffer to save the world. The events of the previous Passover were the fulfilment of all those Scriptures – verse 18.

Therefore, it is time to turn around and take a very different view of life – verse 19. By embracing what God was doing in Jesus, all our sins can be wiped away. The old animal sacrifices have been replaced by the real thing now. The death and resurrection of Jesus, according to the Scriptures, means that not only can the sins of the world be completely forgiven and forgotten, but we can have a deep friendship with the Living God in which we enjoy times of refreshment and joy in His fellowship – verse 19.

The people of Israel and Jerusalem had endured generations of hardship under Roman rule, but now they could find divine refreshment in the divine

---

24   The LORD God is frequently described as the Righteous One or the Holy One – 2 Ki. 19:22; Ps. 71:22; 78:41; 89:18; Isa. 1:4; 5:19, 24; 10:20; 12:6; 17:7; 29:19; 30:11f, 15; 31:1; 37:23; 41:14, 16, 20; 43:3, 14; 45:11; 47:4; 48:17; 49:7; 54:5; 55:5; 60:9, 14; Jer. 50:29; 51:5.

Messiah. Furthermore, Peter explains that Jesus' death and resurrection affect not only the past and the present, but also a bright new future that stretches away into eternity through Jesus. Jesus is waiting in heaven until the day when the Living God will bring restoration and renewal to the whole creation, just as He promised through the prophets. Peter gives one example of Moses prophesying Jesus (Deuteronomy 18:15-19), but he indicates that all the prophets spoke about Jesus and the glorious future He would bring through His suffering – verses 21-24).

Peter was most probably thinking here of Ezekiel's vision of the restored temple or the way Exodus ends with the divine glory flooding the whole tabernacle. Perhaps he was thinking of Daniel 12:2-3 or even Isaiah 65:17-25.

> Behold, I will create new heavens and a new earth. The former things will not be remembered, nor will they come to mind. But be glad and rejoice for ever in what I will create, for I will create Jerusalem to be a delight and its people a joy. I will rejoice over Jerusalem and take delight in my people; the sound of weeping and of crying will be heard in it no more... Before they call I will answer; while they are still speaking I will hear. The wolf and the lamb will feed together, and the lion will eat straw like the ox, but dust will be the serpent's food. They will neither harm nor destroy on all my holy mountain," says the LORD.

All the ancient promises of a resurrection future for the earth are guaranteed by the resurrected and exalted Jesus and simply waiting delivery when He returns.

The Jewish people are first in line to receive all the blessings of Jesus – verses 25-26. They had been prepared for these days by the prophets and the promises made to Abraham. Before it would all be offered to the rest of the world, the God of Abraham wanted to make sure it was first preached to the people who had waited so long for the Promised Messiah – verse 26.

Each person had to turn from their wicked ways and turn to the glorious ways of Jesus – verse 26. The Living God deals with us individually because He cares for each of us individually.

c. Peter and John before the Sanhedrin (4:1-21)

It seems that the priests and the temple guard were under the control of the Sadducees (see Acts 5:17) because once they heard Peter and John speaking about the resurrection of the dead they arrested them. In Acts 23:8, Luke explains more about the weird cult of the Sadducees – "The Sadducees say that there is no resurrection, and that there are neither angels nor spirits".

The Sadducees had clashed with Jesus over this issue of the resurrection (see Matthew 22:23-33) and now they were hearing that Jesus had defied them in the worst possible way by actually being resurrected! It was bad enough when Jesus insisted on talking about resurrection, but now that He actually *was resurrected* it would start to make them look a little bit stupid!

However, many of the people who had heard Peter and John had believed and already there were five thousand adult male Jesus-followers in Jerusalem – verse 4. If we think of all the adult women and children as well, then there may have been 15-20,000 followers of Jesus within days of the ascension!

Luke, being such a careful historian, researched who was present at the gathering of Jewish leaders (verse 6). According to John 18:16, the high priest knew John. These were the very same people who had murdered Jesus and now it must have seemed to them that Jesus was being cloned and multiplied.

They couldn't dispute the fact of the miracle, so they tried to focus on how it was done – verse 7. Presumably they hoped that they could prove that it was done by satanic power. However, Peter was (again) empowered by the Holy Spirit and answered their question – verse 8.

Peter first notes how strange it is that they were arrested, jailed and now questioned about… an act of kindness! (verse 9). They had been able to act so kindly to the lame man because of the name of Jesus the Messiah. They had killed Him in the worst possible way[25] but the Living God had sided with Jesus and resurrected Him (whether they believed in resurrection or not!). Then Peter quotes a very provocative Scripture – Psalm 118:22.

---

25   Remember Deuteronomy 21:22-23

Psalm 118 prophetically acknowledges the salvation of the LORD God as He goes up to the temple in a festival of palm branches (see Luke 19:38). Yet, the Psalm predicted that at the crucial moment when the LORD God is accomplishing His salvation, the leaders/builders of the nation will reject Him! The Psalm celebrates the fact that the Messiah was not abandoned to death but resurrected in great triumph over His enemies. Even though the leaders reject the saving LORD God, still He will be the stone that holds everything together, the One that gives the building its strength.[26]

Psalm 118:14 proclaimed "The LORD is my strength and my song; he has become my salvation." Peter stands on that truth and insists that the LORD of Psalm 118 is none other than Jesus of Nazareth – "Salvation is found in no-one else, for there is no other name under heaven given to men by which we must be saved."

In Hebrew Psalm 118:14 is "The LORD is my strength and my song; he has become my *Y'shua* (Jesus)".[27]

Peter could hardly be more direct. The leaders were amazed that such an excellent point of Biblical scholarship was made by these uneducated men – Acts 4:13. Just as Jesus had silenced them with His answers, now the same was happening with His followers. Far from getting rid of Jesus the Cornerstone, He has being replicated in more and more people. The life and character of Jesus was shining through Peter and John – "They took note that these men had been with Jesus"- verse 13.

May that always be true of us as well. Whether people agree with all we say or not, they must always know what Jesus is really like by the fact that we live and speak just like Him. As we spend time with Jesus, treasuring His teaching and following His steps, so we will live just as Jesus lived.

If we trust Him then we will be like Him.

We cannot glibly say, "don't look at me, just look at Jesus", because the only way people can see Jesus is by looking at us.

---

26   In Isaiah 19:13 we see that the cornerstones/capstones of a society are the key leaders.

27   For more on this please visit the Jews for Jesus website – www.jewsforjesus.org

The leaders of the Sanhedrin were facing a difficulty. They couldn't deny that the man had been wondrously healed. Everybody knew about it. Peter had taken a very radical stand, making it clear that Jesus alone was the power behind everything they did. That is why the Sanhedrin's words of verses 17-18 are so futile and ridiculous. If Jesus is the LORD God and there is salvation in no one other than Jesus, then how could they silence such a glorious truth?

Peter and John put this point to them in simple terms – verses 19-20. If this is true (and they were eye-witnesses of the fact), then it would be sinful to be silent.

How bizarre that the religious leaders find themselves trying to punish two men for causing all the people to praise God – verse 21. This is the spiritual blindness that hides behind human religion and ideology. Faced with no other options they have to release Peter and John – verse 23.

d. The Believers' Prayer (4:23-31)

How would the Jesus movement respond to this official opposition? Would they be intimidated? Would careful and cautious voices argue for a more careful and cautious approach? Would they call a halt until they had been able to persuade more of the religious leadership?

The response seems to have been unanimous because they all began to pray together.

They begin by recognising that their Father in heaven has absolute sovereignty over the whole creation. He made everything and can do whatever He likes with it all – verse 24. They remind the Father that His own Scriptures predict that the nations and leaders always unite against Jesus in Psalm 2:1-2 – verses 25-26. They tell the Father that they had seen David's prophecy come true when Herod and Pilate led the Jews and the Gentiles in opposition to Jesus the Messiah – verse 27.

Nevertheless, given that the Father is sovereign over everything, then even this opposition is under His control and they could only do what He purposed that they should do! If the opposition was allowed to murder Jesus, then there is no point in praying that the followers of Jesus will be exempt from opposition. They must follow where Jesus leads. So, concerning the opponents of Jesus, all that the apostolic churches ask is that He would "consider their threats" – verse 29.

Their main concern, however, was that they would not fail in the mission that Jesus had set for them. Faced with such influential opposition they realised that they might start to become intimidated and try to keep a low profile.

> Now, Lord, consider their threats and enable your servants to speak your word with great boldness. Stretch out your hand to heal and perform miraculous signs and wonders through the name of your holy servant Jesus.

In other words, they wanted to make sure that they drew even more attention to what they were doing and saying so that the Name of Jesus would be lifted up even more.

Later we see the Apostle Paul adopt the same attitude. In 1 Thessalonians 2:1, Paul is describing his time in Philippi, Berea and Thessalonica where on each occasion he was opposed or beaten or people tried to kill him. To Paul this was not a failure. Failure would have been lacking the confidence to continue speaking about Jesus. God helped Paul then in the same way as he helps the Apostles here, to continue to proclaim the gospel with boldness, despite this opposition.

May we always have that instinct in our prayers. May we also recognise where the weakness and danger might lie and pray for ways to take the initiative. It is never enough for us to simply defend our position. We need to find ways to lift up the Name of Jesus in our lives, in our societies, in our work, in our neighbourhoods. What would show the people around us that Jesus is the LORD God and that salvation is in Him alone? Do those who meet us realise that we have been with Jesus, that we are like Him in the way we live and serve and love?

Their prayer was answered and they were baptised/filled with the Spirit yet again – verse 31. It was just as if the day of Pentecost was happening all over again and they "spoke the word of God boldly".

Study 3   Bible Questions

Acts 4:1-22

1. Verses 1-2 – What specifically bothered the religious leaders according to these verses? Why is this such a problem? Do we cause the same reaction when we talk about Jesus? Why?

2. Verses 3-4 – Why would people believe the accounts given by Peter and John, especially bearing in mind they had been put in prison?

3. Verses 5-6 – Why does Luke want us to know who was present at this meeting the next morning? Where have we heard these names before?

4. Verse 7 – In light of the miracle that had been performed in chapter 3, why is the question of the religious leaders in verse 7 so strange? What were they trying to achieve?

5. Verse 8 – What does this verse tell us about being filled with the Holy Spirit?

6. Verse 9 – How does Peter describe the miracle of the previous day?

7. Verses 10-11 – In what ways does Peter directly challenge the leaders in front of him? What does this tell us about Peter's intention as he spoke?

8. Verses 12 – What does this verse tell us about the name of Jesus? How does this fit with the way our world views this name?

9. Verses 13-17 – What did the leaders notice about Peter and John? How can we ensure that people notice the same of us? What conclusion did the religious leaders reach concerning the miracle?

10. Verses 18-22 – What is the central issue being addressed in these verses? What two reactions are described in these verses and what do they tell us about the way of Jesus?

11. Verses 1-22 – What can we learn about our own evangelism from the example of Peter and John in these verses?

Study 3   Further Questions

Why would the healing of the beggar at the Beautiful Gate have had such an impact? Were Peter and John looking for notoriety by this act? Why did they pick on this man and not the many other people in need of healing that may have been present?

We are told that Peter and John had great courage as a result of being filled with the Holy Spirit and because they had been with Jesus. How do these two factors affect us in our daily lives and in our outreach? How are we different to Peter and John.?

How could our church fellowships more closely mirror the fellowship of the believers described in Acts 4:32-37? What could you do today to be a part of this radical lifestyle and promote it to others in your Fellowship group?

Study 3	Daily Readings
Day 1	Acts 3
Day 2	Acts 4
Day 3	Psalm 2
Day 4	Psalm 118
Day 5	Nehemiah 5
Day 6	Matthew 22:23-33
Day 7	2 Peter 1:12-21

The daily Bible readings are an opportunity to not only read through all of the material in the book under study, but also to read parts of the Bible that relate to the themes and issues that we have been considering. We try to make sure that we receive light from the whole Bible as we think through the key issues each week.

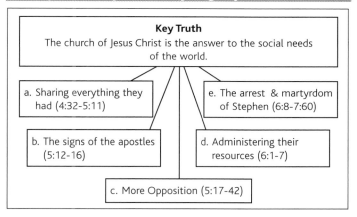

Key Truth
The church of Jesus Christ is the answer to the social needs of the world.

a. Sharing everything they had (4:32-5:11)

e. The arrest & martyrdom of Stephen (6:8-7:60)

b. The signs of the apostles (5:12-16)

d. Administering their resources (6:1-7)

c. More Opposition (5:17-42)

a. Sharing everything they had (4:32-5:11)

The healing of the lame man had helped people to see the power of the Name of Jesus, but a much bigger and more fundamental miracle was also happening. Since the beginning of the world thinkers and leaders have tried to find a way to solve the problems of social injustice and need. How can we all live together with love and freedom, justice and compassion?

Where the philosophers and politicians have failed, the Risen and Ascended Jesus triumphs. The salvation in the Name of Jesus is far more than eternal fire insurance. The LORD Jesus saves those who follow Him not only from a future judgement but also from the selfish ways that have provoked that future judgement. Jesus saves us from the materialism, pride and greed that lie behind so many of the world's problems. He gives us His eternal life of love, peace, contentment and generosity to replace the way of death that we have followed for too long.[28]

---

28   The Didache is a document written sometime around 50AD, before the New Testament books were written, and it is a fascinating insight into that very early understanding of the good news of Jesus. There is the way of life and the way of death – and they are extremely different. Jesus leads us on the way of life, which leads to resurrection when He returns. We know that we will live with Him when He returns because we live His way right now.

The church of Jesus Christ is the answer to the social needs of the world.

> All the believers were one in heart and mind. No-one claimed that any of his possessions was his own, but they shared everything they had. With great power the apostles continued to testify to the resurrection of the Lord Jesus, and much grace was upon them all. There were no needy persons among them. For from time to time those who owned lands or houses sold them, brought the money from the sales and put it at the apostles' feet, and it was distributed to anyone as he had need.

It is well worth spending time carefully studying and memorising this description of the Way of Jesus. This was the Way that turned the ancient world upside down and it will turn our communities and our nations, the modern world, upside down as well. There is always a great temptation to reduce the way of Jesus to some theory about soul-salvation or to some kind of church ghetto or even pervert it into a way to be healthy and wealthy. However, whenever the followers of Jesus have grasped the true and original Way of Jesus, only then does the revolution of Jesus happen.

First, the believers were one in heart and mind. Too often we try to create this in advance of obeying Jesus, but all the evidence of the Bible and history shows us that this unity of heart and mind come about when we are working/walking together in the Way of Jesus. When we are standing shoulder to shoulder trying to live as Jesus lived, sharing all we have, caring for those in need, explaining the glorious birth, life, death, resurrection and ascension of Jesus… then we find that so many of the things we argued about have fallen into a proper perspective.[29]

Second, Jesus' teaching about possessions was taken seriously. Jesus claimed that it is impossible to serve both God and money/possessions. He warned that if we try to store up treasure and security on earth we will have no heavenly future. He taught that our hearts will follow our investment strategy, that our hearts will perish with this passing age if that is where our treasure and security lies.

---

29   This is not to say that there are never genuine and vital theological arguments. The apostle Paul is forced to confront serious threats to the Way of Jesus within that early apostolic community. However, we will see so much more clearly what is a real threat and what is mere opinion when all our strength and purpose is focussed on living as Jesus lived with all those who are trying to do the same.

Those that trusted Jesus in Acts 4:32-35 knew that all they possessed had come from the Living God and would all be taken from them in the end. Nothing really belongs to us at all and we need to live this out in the Way of Jesus. Yes, we may continue to look after our car, our house, our computer, our kitchen, our resources. Yet all these things are for the use of others. They are to be shared as the need arises.

A friend challenged me that we should never own anything that we are not happy to give away. Those words come back to me nearly every day. Everything I have belongs to Jesus, so how can I ever claim anything as my own? If I decide that I really need to retain something for my work or my family responsibilities, then shouldn't I explain that thinking to my brothers and sisters in Jesus to get their permission to do that?

It is no surprise that in such a glorious social expression of the reality of the Risen Jesus, the apostles "continued to testify to the resurrection of the Lord Jesus, and much grace was upon them all" (verse 33). People may argue with our words, but how can they argue with such a potent demonstration of the resurrection of Jesus?

Acts 4:32 begins with one of the most remarkable statements in the whole Bible – "There were no needy persons among them." This is the fulfilment of the Law of Moses of Deuteronomy 15:4 – "there should be no poor among you".

We live in a world of terrible injustice and greed. There are always poor people around us, as Deuteronomy 15:10-11[30] acknowledges and Jesus confirms in Matthew 26:11 and Mark 14:7. However, within the community of Jesus, as a global community, there should be no needy among us. As 2 Corinthians 8 teaches, when there is famine and need in one area, the brothers and sisters in other areas send all the help they can spare. The LORD God has provided enough for everybody in the world… if only we will share all we have.

The needy were cared for not by a centralised gathering of all resources, but "from time to time those who owned lands or houses sold them, brought the

---

30   "Give generously to (your needy brothers and sisters) and do so without a grudging heart; then because of this the LORD your God will bless you in all your work and in everything you put your hand to. There will always be poor people in the land. Therefore I command you to be open-handed towards your brothers and towards the poor and needy in your land." Deuteronomy 15:10-11.

money from the sales and put it at the apostles' feet, and it was distributed to anyone as he had need" (verse 34-35). There is a wonderful balance here. This is not a Marxist revolution where the centre takes control of all property in the name of society. No, there is no abandonment of personal generosity and compassion to the state. Nor is there a denial of personal property as such. Each person retained the care of their property and they only sold it if as specific need arose.

The Living God gives us money and property and possessions in order to give each of us opportunities to show the reality of Jesus in how we administer these things. It would be wrong to remove these opportunities for personal growth and sacrifice by simply taking all property into a centralised pot.

In every age we need to feel the challenge of these verses. How this might look in all the different cultures and ages of the world will certainly vary. However, we should never be any less radical than they were in our generosity and compassion. We should always be encouraging each other to share more, to give more, to serve more, to be more and more like Jesus.

We cannot win the world for Jesus if we basically live the same way as everybody else.

At this stage the apostles managed all the distribution to the needy and with so many thousands of people in the community we can already see why they needed to find people who would take over that aspect of the work – see Acts chapter 6.

Acts 4 ends by introducing us to a Levite from Cyprus called Joseph, but more commonly known as Barnabas – the son of encouragement. He will play a vital role in the story that Luke is telling us, but for now we simply see that he was an authentic example of the way of Jesus in those days. He had a field, saw the urgent social needs and realised that the best use of his property was to sell it and put the money into the hands of the apostles for those who had need.

However, by contrast, we are immediately shown the opposite example of Ananias and Sapphira. Their names are beautiful (Ananias – gracious gift; Sapphira – named after the precious stone that characterises the divine pavement – Exodus 24:20), but their lives and character were ugly.

They also sold a property and claimed that they were giving the entire proceeds of the sale to the apostles. However, secretly they retained some of the money for their own use.

The problem here was not that they retained some of the money, but that they lied about it. The property was theirs to do with what they pleased, as Peter explains in 5:4-5. They could keep it all, give 50% or give 100%. In a community of such love and purity, when the reality of Jesus and the Spirit was so evident, to introduce such hypocrisy and deceit was blasphemy. We have seen the close identity between the apostles and Jesus Himself, so to lie to the apostles was equivalent to lying to the Holy Spirit. They might be able to deceive mere human beings, but we dare not bring such deceit and corruption into the presence of the Spirit.

Peter gave Sapphira a chance to repent, but she was so tied into her greed that she thought she could deceive both humans and the Spirit – verses 7-9. We may be shocked at the fatal character of this church discipline, but we see the same thing happen in 1 Corinthians 11:30 when the Corinthians brought their divisions and greed into their shared thanksgiving meal.

The same Spirit who disciplined His church then will discipline us today. We sometimes pray for revival and purity in the church, but such a spiritual awakening will bring this same requirement of integrity and honesty. How would we stand if the Spirit was really present in that way in our own church? Would any of us be left alive?

Fear gripped the church then (verse 11) and surely that same fear of the Living Holy God is desperately needed in the church today.

b. The signs of the apostles (5:12-16)

Throughout these chapters of Luke's history we are very aware of the power and presence of the Spirit among the followers of the resurrected Jesus.

Jesus had appointed the apostles to be His eye-witnesses of all they had seen from the time of Jesus' baptism right through to Jesus' ascension into heaven. In order to constantly demonstrate that their eye-witness accounts were authorised by heaven itself, remarkable signs and wonders surrounded the apostles in those days. Only in the ministry of Jesus Himself do we read of such extraordinary demonstration of the Spirit's power.

…people brought the sick into the streets and laid them on beds and mats so that at least Peter's shadow might fall on some of them as he passed by. Crowds gathered also from the towns around Jerusalem, bringing their sick and those tormented by evil spirits, and all of them were healed (Acts 5:15-16)

When we see this incredible authentication of the original apostles we can see why they have such a unique place in the history of the church. When the apostle John was shown a vision of the City of God in Revelation 21:14 – "The wall of the city had twelve foundations, and on them were the names of the twelve apostles of the Lamb."

People in the church today sometimes call themselves apostles and there may be certain senses in which that might be possible. Indeed people other than the twelve are described as apostles elsewhere in the Bible, for example Acts 14:14, possibly Romans 16:7. However, nobody can ever claim to have the foundational authority that those original apostles had. In a profound and unique way they acted with the authority and power of Jesus Himself.

The power and purity and generosity of the community of Jesus followers was such that paradoxically people were too frightened to join but just had to join them anyway – verse 13-14. Every day, in fear and trembling, men and women began to follow Jesus in life and heart. The church was highly regarded by ordinary people, just as Jesus had been – Mark 12:37.

Please, Lord Jesus, have mercy on us for our impurity and hypocrisy. Forgive us for the bad reputation that we have so often acquired for judgementalism and self-righteousness. Please restore us. Please send your Spirit to judge us and purify us, even if it means that some of us won't survive the process. Lord Jesus, restore your church at all costs and let the world see your light and glory.

c. More Opposition (5:17-42)

So often religious conflicts come down to jealousy and that was certainly the case when the temple leaders saw what was happening in Jerusalem. People tend to dress these things up in theological language and pious words, but underneath it is always just gross and selfish sin.

The temple authorities wanted to be number one. They wanted to determine what was right and wrong, who was acceptable and who was not. They wanted the people to listen to them. They were jealous for what did not belong to them.[31]

The apostles were arrested and imprisoned again – verse 18. However, this time an angel was sent from heaven to break them out of jail. Instead of advising them to keep a low profile the message from the throneroom of the universe was "Go, stand in the temple courts and tell the people the full message of this new life" – verse 20.

On some occasions, Jesus' followers are miraculously freed from imprisonment and opposition as they are here, on other occasions they are not as in the previous chapter. This reminds us that the LORD God is in charge and knows what is the best outcome of any given situation.

Notice that the angel summarised the gospel as "the full message of this new life". The followers of Jesus were living a radically new kind of life and they had to tell everyone the truth that generated this new life. The gospel is both the message and the new life – one without the other gives a false impression. We need to use words to preach, but if our words are not matched by our lives then we bring dishonour and shame on the Name of Jesus.

The religious leaders were selfish in their jealousy, but the apostles were self-sacrificial to bring this new life of Jesus to the world.

In the morning the apostles obediently went to preach at the temple, which caused total confusion among the temple leaders when they couldn't find them in the prison – verses 21-24. Eventually somebody told them where the apostles were – verse 25. The reality of Jesus was so obvious to the crowds that the temple guards had to be very careful about removing the apostles. Now the temple party was in danger of being accused of blasphemy and stoned for it – verse 26.

---

31 The LORD God is a jealous God – Exodus 20:5, because He is jealous for the things that belong to Him. A woman is rightly jealous if her husband's love is given to another. That love belongs to her. However, if she were to be jealous for the love of a man who was married to someone else, then that would be an evil jealousy. In Acts 5 the apostles had the authority of the Name of Jesus and the temple leaders were jealous of that. They wanted what belongs to Jesus alone.

Faced by those who feared God rather than humans, the powerlessness of the Sanhedrin was apparent. They locked the men up, but now they were free. They banned them from speaking about Jesus, but now the whole of Jerusalem was ringing with the Name of Jesus. Trying to accuse others of blasphemy, they find themselves in danger of that very accusation.

Notice how their consciences accused them – "(you) are determined to make us guilty of this man's blood" (verse 28). They were already guilty of Jesus' blood as they had actually admitted in Matthew 27:25.

In reply, Peter gives essentially the same message he has preached before. How could they obey the religious leaders who had killed Jesus by the cursed death[32] when the Living God had vindicated Jesus in resurrection? Jesus had been exalted to the highest heaven not to destroy Israel, but to turn Israel's life around as He forgave their sins. Yes, that cursed death on the tree had actually made atonement for Israel and now a new beginning was offered by the crucified and risen Saviour!

This message was not only backed by the apostolic eye witnesses, but also by God the Spirit Himself! The fact that the temple authorities don't hear the witness of God's Spirit proves that they are not obeying Him – verse 32.

Such a direct word of truth, such a beam of light into the darkness, had to bring immediate repentance or furious rejection... and it was the latter in this case – verse 33.

Before things got out of hand a wise teacher called Gamaliel offered some wisdom. This is the man who had been the tutor of Saul of Tarsus (Acts 22:3), proving that Paul must have studied in Jerusalem for some time. If that is the case, then it seems certain that Paul must have seen and heard Jesus.

Gamaliel pointed out that human revolutions always fail and burn out. On the other hand, a divine revolution cannot be resisted. Either way they did not need to do anything about the Way of Jesus. If it was human it would die out, but if it was divine it could not be stopped – verses 34-39.

As we look back on all the events from Acts 4:32, the mighty power of the Living God has been demonstrated in so many ways. Luke has shown us which

---

32   See Deuteronomy 21:22-23

part of Gamaliel's wisdom was relevant to the Way of Jesus!

However, even with this wisdom, in a cruel and evil way, the Sanhedrin had to try to impose their vacuous authority and had the apostles flogged – verse 40. Again, in spite of Gamaliel's wisdom, they tried to order the apostles not to speak about Jesus – verse 40.

Yet, far from silencing the Jesus movement, the apostles just carried on more than ever, not only in the temple but also now in the houses of ordinary people. Because this was from the Living God it could not be stopped.

The apostles left the Sanhedrin, rejoicing because they had been counted worthy of suffering disgrace for the Name.

The Name of Jesus was so wonderful, so precious, so glorious, so highly exalted to those apostolic Christians that they were jumping for joy when they realised that they had been counted worthy of suffering disgrace for that Name. They were experiencing the joy that Jesus described at the beginning of His mighty sermon – Matthew 5:10-12.

d. Administering their resources (6:1-7)

The apostles were obviously overworked. Not only were they publicly teaching but they were also managing all the social needs of the new community. For example, the Hebrew Jews were presumably based in Jerusalem and had more access to these social resources, whereas the Gentile converts to Judaism were not properly linked into the system – verse 1.

The Twelve asked the believers to find seven men who could give special attention to the social care of the community – verses 2-4. Although this was essentially a very practical role the men had to be full of the Spirit as well as full of practical wisdom – verse 3.

This is very important. In local churches all around the world there have been so many terrible disasters because ungodly, immature people have been appointed into 'practical' roles involving money, buildings and care. Church divisions, financial mess, abuse of trust, loss of reputation and serious mismanagement happen all too often because the basic lessons of Acts 6 are not learned. With the practical skills and wisdom, there has to be the godliness and maturity. In these first chapters of Acts we have already seen how the honour and glory of Jesus' Name was so tied up with the integrity and generosity of the community. No church can ever afford to put anybody in any leadership position – whether practical or pastoral – unless they are proven as mature Spirit-filled servants of Jesus.

They found seven suitable men and appointed them to the work – verse 6 – and the result was a further increase in the community, especially among the priests – verse 7. The fact that the priests from the temple left the Sadducees and joined the followers of Jesus is such an important footnote to the conflicts we have studied. As the apostles suffered opposition, they continued to faithfully witness to Jesus in the Way that Jesus had shown them in His own suffering. The apostolic care for people rather than the Sadducee's selfish jealousy had all proved to this large number of priests that Jesus really is the Way, the Truth and the Life.

e. The arrest and martyrdom of Stephen (6:8-7:60)

One of the newly appointed administrators was called Stephen and he was a remarkable example of godliness, wisdom and maturity. He was full miraculous gifts of the Spirit – verse 8. Inevitably, such fruitful and godly witness for Jesus will attract the most severe opposition and in Stephen's case it came from a strange group called "The Synagogue of the Freedman".

It is very hard to determine exactly who and what these Jews were, but it seems that they had their own dedicated synagogue in the Jerusalem area. From their name it is possible they were slaves who had been granted their freedom. According to Acts 2:11, Cyrene is in North Africa, and the same is true of Alexandria. So, this group of possibly Gentile converts to Judaism came from right across North Africa and Turkey/Asia Minor.

They had the fanaticism of the convert when it came to the things of Moses and when they heard the apostles explaining how Jesus was the one that Moses was writing about, the One who had fulfilled all that the Law prophesied, they took very great offence – verses 13-14. They stirred up trouble among the people and captured Stephen. As far as they were concerned nobody could be greater than Moses... not even the Messiah that Moses was writing about!

Stephen's very appearance seemed to reflect how heavenly this wonderful servant of Jesus was – 6:15 – and the fact that at the end of his speech he is able to gaze directly into heaven gives us a sense of how close he walked with Jesus.

Stephen's explanation of the situation is a brilliant speech. The accusation against him was that he spoke against the temple and against Moses. His whole speech is a Biblical vindication against those accusations.

Stephen's defence with respect to *Moses* is necessarily lengthy – Acts 7:2-43. He begins by showing that he knows the writings of Moses in great detail. He accurately and brilliantly summarises the content of the first two books of Moses. Yet, on the way he makes important points. First, he notes how Abraham himself did not get any of the promised land – verses 4-5. To be so passionate about the land of Israel and the temple of Jerusalem is not the way of Abraham. Furthermore, Abraham was told that his descendants would spend a lot of time far away from the promised land – verses 6-8.

Joseph, the model man of God in the book of Genesis, was rejected by his brothers and lived away from the promised land in Egypt – verses 9-16. In all this Stephen is showing his opponents that their zeal for the land and the temple is not what Moses was teaching at all. If they were faithful to Moses then they would see beyond the land and the temple to the reality of the Messiah and His new creation future.[33]

Stephen is very careful when he comes to the story of Moses – verses 20-43. In verses 20-22 he shows the excellent qualities of Moses, before God and in human terms.

From verse 23 Stephen introduces a new, subtle note. Moses was attempting to deliver God's people from slavery but they rejected him asking, "who made you a ruler and judge over us?". Stephen wants to establish that the Jewish people were not always on the side of Moses, according to the Scriptures.

In verses 30-36, Stephen carefully describes how Moses was personally appointed by the LORD God Himself at the burning bush. The Jews may have questioned who made him ruler, but the answer to that question was "the

---

33   Just as Abraham did – see Hebrews 11:8-16.

LORD God Himself"! (verse 35). With this divine authority with him, Moses delivered the people from slavery even if they were unsure about him and rebelled against him. Far from undermining Moses, Stephen was showing the incredible authority and approval given to Moses by the LORD God, even when the people had grumbled against Moses (verse 39).

Moses had spoken with the divine angel at Mount Sinai (verse 38) and prophesied that there would be another prophet like him in the future. How could Stephen be accused of rejecting Moses when he was simply announcing that Moses' prophecy had come true?

Stephen wants to make it very clear that most of Israel has always turned away from the Living God and His prophets. They may have appeared to be 'religious' and 'zealous', yet their hearts were full of unbelief and rebellion. This was definitively proved when Moses went up the mountain to get the Law. While he was away the religious leaders of the people actually led the people into the worship of a golden calf, a man-made object – verse 41.

Stephen's point here is very direct. These Jewish leaders and their Gentile convert zealots, had mistaken that man-made temple for the LORD God Himself who had been among them! In their day it was the temple, but in the days of Moses it had been the golden calf. Stephen drives his point even harder when he quotes from the prophet Amos. This worship of man-made creatures is actually the most foul and abominable worship of pagan deities and demons – Amos 5:25-27.

With respect to the *temple* (Acts 7:44-50), Stephen notes that the original building had been a simple tent made according to the pattern given to Moses in the desert. Indeed throughout his defence, Stephen has demonstrated that the Living God was not tied to any earthly structure or location but was always where his people were at, whether that was Mesopotamia, Egypt, or Jerusalem. This was made crystal clear as the tabernacle of the testimony moved with the people – God on the move. This tabernacle had been carried around and even neglected until the time of David. David wanted to build a temple but was not permitted. Even when Solomon was allowed to build the temple the Lord God Himself put the temple into a proper perspective in Isaiah 66:1-2, quoting 1 Kings 8:27-30. In other words, Stephen notes that in exalting so highly that earthly temple built by Herod, these religious leaders were actually rebelling against the Living God who cannot even be contained by the heavens that God Himself made!

All of this leads to Stephen's damning conclusion. These so-called zealots for the temple and the Law are actually uncircumcised pagans (verse 51), who reject the Holy Spirit. They stand in that long tradition of rebellious, devil-worshipping murderers who litter the history of Israel. Finally, having killed or opposed all the godly prophets down the ages, they had killed the very One that all the prophets spoke about – The Righteous One, the Promised Messiah.

Having been so comprehensively exposed, the temple authorities show their true colours, behaving like wild animals.

Stephen is counted worthy of dying at their hands just as his Lord and Saviour Jesus. Stephen is enabled to see the glory of God and Jesus Himself standing, ready to welcome Stephen into His presence. Bearing witness to this only causes the evil leaders to flee further into the darkness and they drag him outside the city to kill him.

Just as Jesus had done, Stephen not only asks forgiveness for his murderers – verse 60, but also gives his spirit into the hands of the Living God – verse 59.

Watching it all, holding the coats of the murderers, was a young man called Saul – verse 58 and 8:1.

Study 4	Bible Questions

Acts 6:12-15 and 7:44-60

1. Verses 12-15 – What form has the opposition to the gospel and to the believers taken in the preceding chapters? What form does the opposition take in this section? What does this tell us?

2. Verses 44-46 – How had the tabernacle been made and why was this important? See also Hebrews 8:5. What did the portability of the tabernacle signify for the people of God?

3. Verses 47-50 – What was great about the temple that Solomon built and in what ways, according to Stephen was it limited? What sort of a mistake is it to be consumed with the Temple but to ignore the God who it points to? How might people make the same mistake today?

4. Verses 51-53 – In what ways were Stephen's accusers resisting the Holy Spirit? Who else was guilty of the same attitude in the Bible? Who is guilty of this attitude today? What is Stephen hoping for as he speaks in the way he does?

5. Verse 54 – What is the difference in response to Stephen's speech here, compared to Peter's speech in Acts 2? Why is this?

6. Verses 55-56 – Why was Stephen given this vision at this time? What did such a vision mean to Stephen's accusers? What does it mean to us?

7. Verses 57-58 – Describe the mood and the actions of Stephen's accusers in these verses? Why does Luke tell us about Saul and his role in the event here?

8. Verses 59-60 – How is Stephen's death similar to Jesus' death? How does Luke describe the moment that Stephen died? Why?

9. Verses 44-60 – What do the words and actions of Stephen in this section tell us about his attitude to the gospel message? What can and should we learn from Stephen?

Study 4   Further Questions

What does chapter 6 tell us about the daily life of the church at that time and about the nature of people chosen to carry out the so called "practical" jobs in the church? How can we adopt a similar approach in our churches?

Why does Stephen refer to the Divine Angel of the Old Testament as merely "an angel" in Acts 7:30? What does this section of Stephen's speech tell us about what Moses knew and understood?

What was the point of Solomon building the Temple if the Living God could never be contained in any building, however magnificent? How might we make a similar mistake to the religious leaders in connection with our church buildings? Are prayers offered in church are more significant or more likely to be heard than prayers offered elsewhere? Why?

Study 4   Daily Readings

Day 1	Acts 4:32-5:16
Day 2	Acts 5:17-42
Day 3	Acts 6
Day 4	Acts 7:1-43
Day 5	Acts 7:44-60
Day 6	Exodus 3
Day 7	1 Kings 8:22-53

The daily Bible readings are an opportunity to not only read through all of the material in the book under study, but also to read parts of the Bible that relate to the themes and issues that we have been considering. We try to make sure that we receive light from the whole Bible as we think through the key issues each week.

Death of Saul

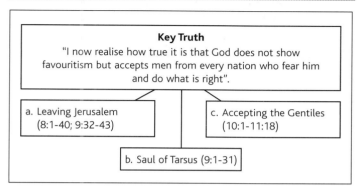

Key Truth
"I now realise how true it is that God does not show favouritism but accepts men from every nation who fear him and do what is right".

a. Leaving Jerusalem (8:1-40; 9:32-43)

c. Accepting the Gentiles (10:1-11:18)

b. Saul of Tarsus (9:1-31)

a.   Leaving Jerusalem (8:1-40; 9:32-43)

Jesus had given his apostles a very specific commission just before He ascended to rule the universe: "you will be my witnesses in Jerusalem, and in all Judea and Samaria, and to the ends of the earth" (Acts 1:8). The first two steps may seem small to us, yet they held great significance for that community of Jesus-followers.

Witnessing to Jesus in Jerusalem seemed almost impossible.

How would they manage in wider Judea?

How could they possibly take this revolutionary new life to the people of a different religion like the people of Samaria?

To take this to the unknown and incredibly diverse nations of the whole earth was surely beyond all imagination and fantasy?!

The murder of Stephen unleashed a wave of violent opposition to the Way of Jesus. Only the apostles were able to stand firm against it. The thousands of other followers of Jesus were scattered out around the region of Judea and Samaria (verse 1). Perhaps without even realising it, they had fulfilled the first three parts of Jesus' commission!

That young man called Saul, who had witnessed the murder of Stephen, "began to destroy the church" (verse 3). With all his religious zeal he tried to imprison anyone who followed Jesus.

Another of the appointed administrators was a man called Philip who escaped from the persecution to a city in Samaria. Just as Jesus had made a strong impression on the followers of the Samaritan religion, so Philip did too.[34] They may have been intimidated by the idea of taking the Way of Jesus to a different religion and yet Jesus brought great joy to that Samaritan city.[35]

However, in crossing cultural boundaries for Jesus there will always be those with vested interests who do not want the freedom of new life in Jesus. It was true in Jerusalem and it was also true in Samaria. It will be true wherever you live as you study the book of Acts today.

Simon the sorcerer was known as "The Great Power" in Samaria. Because of his magical powers he was thought to be some kind of god. He liked to boast about himself – verses 9-11. In the writings of the early generations of Christians after the apostles, Simon Magus was known as one of the leading Gnostic teachers of the first century.[36]

If Jerusalem had been marked by a clash of religious leaders, in Samaria it was a clash of spiritual powers.

---

34   See John chapter 4, especially verses 39-42.

35   In many ways the Samaritans were like a halfway position between the Jews and the Gentiles. The Samaritans accepted the Law of Moses and were waiting for the Messiah, yet they rejected Jerusalem and the temple. In many ways the nearest modern equivalent would be Islam, which also shares so many Biblical stories and characters.

36   In Book 1 of Ireneus' work *Against Heresies*, chapter 23 is devoted to the life and heresies of Simon Magus. He writes "This man, then, was glorified by many as if he were a God; and he taught that it was himself who appeared among the Jews as the Son, but descended in Samaria as the Father while he came to other nations in the character of the Holy Spirit. He represented himself, in a word, as being the loftiest of all powers, that is, the Being who is the Father over all, and he allowed himself to be called by whatsoever title men were pleased to address him. 2. Now this Simon of Samaria, from whom all sorts of heresies derive their origin, formed his sect out of the following materials: – Having redeemed from slavery at Tyre, a city of Phoenicia, a certain woman named Helena, he was in the habit of carrying her about with him, declaring that this woman was the first conception of his mind, the mother of all, by whom, in the beginning, he conceived in his mind (the thought) of forming angels and archangels."

When men and women began to follow Jesus, Simon joined the crowd. Simon knew something about spiritual power and he could recognise that there was a kind of power in Philip on a totally different level to anything Simon had ever seen. Simon 'believed and was baptised', yet it soon became clear that Simon's faith was in the miraculous power rather than Jesus. Simon had not turned away from his old way of life at all.

The apostles in Jerusalem heard what was happening and sent Peter and John. On the original day of Pentecost they had all seen something of the international character of the new life in Jesus. However, they needed to see this reinforced in the test case of Samaria.

Could it really be true that the Holy Spirit of the LORD God of Israel would be given to pagan Samaritans? Could the Spirit really live within people who had not become Jewish?

In order to show this incredible truth, there was another 'Pentecost' experience for the new believers in Samaria – verses 15-17. It must have been such a cultural and religious shock to Peter and John. When we remember the words of John 4:9, they must have been stunned to witness these Spirit-filled Samaritans!

The LORD Jesus graciously and carefully led His Jewish people out from behind the fallen wall of the Law into the wide, wide pagan world beyond.

Simon the sorcerer also saw what was happening and now revealed his true colours – verses 18-19. He wanted to buy the power and authority of the apostles! Knowing the way of Jesus, Simon's request is so perversely ridiculous as Peter replies in verses 20-23. Peter urges Simon to repent and seek forgiveness, yet Simon truly was a captive of sin. Instead of doing what Peter instructed, Simon simply told Peter to pray for him instead.

The foolishness of Simon had not stopped the spread of Jesus' new life. In fact, Peter and John were inspired to share the message with other Samaritan villages as they went back to Jerusalem – verse 25.

Philip had done so well in going from Jerusalem through Judea to Samaria, that the Lord Jesus took him onto the final stage of the mission – "the rest of the earth". Philip was sent by an angel onto the road running from Jerusalem through Gaza (in the south) towards Egypt and Ethiopia. Jesus wanted His new life to go to Ethiopia. At this stage Jesus had brought the Ethiopian to Israel, but it wouldn't be long before these apostles would follow these trade routes into all these foreign lands.

There was a long history between Ethiopia and Israel. Moses had married an Ethiopian back in Numbers 12. Then in 1 Kings 10:1-13 we read how the great Ethiopian queen came to visit Solomon. She learned about the LORD God and it seems that a deep connection between the two nations was formed. Perhaps ever since the time of Solomon, the Ethiopian officials had come to Jerusalem to worship the Living God.

This Ethiopian chancellor was reading Isaiah 53, especially verses 7-8. When Philip asked the Ethiopian acknowledged his need of a good Bible teacher.[37] He wanted to know whether the prophet was speaking about himself or someone else – verse 34.[38] Philip was able to explain Isaiah's meaning, telling him all about Jesus (cf. John 12:41).

In Philip's explanation he must have taught the need for repentance and baptism because the Ethiopian stopped the chariot by some water to be baptised. Philip was happy to baptise him right then and there. This is important because in many modern churches a person is forced to go through all kinds of "baptismal preparation classes" before they are allowed to join the Christian community. This is a serious departure from the apostolic practice. If a convert confesses Jesus as Lord then they should be baptised as quickly as possible.

The Ethiopian was a eunuch which meant, according to Deuteronomy 23:1, that he would not be welcome in the assembly (Greek LXX – 'church').[39]

---

37 We must always maintain the balance between acknowledging the essential simplicity of the Bible whereby even the simplest person may become wise as they read it and acknowledging the incredible blessing of the Bible teaching gifts that the Spirit gives. We need the gifts of others if we are going to really open up all the rich treasures of the Bible.

38 It is interesting that this same question so often continues to be asked of the Messianic prophecies even today! Many scholars still wonder if the prophets were only speaking about themselves even if the words were later taken to be applicable to Jesus. Surely the original author's intent is the proper meaning of the Bible. That is to say, if the prophet did not intend to speak about Jesus then it would not be true exegesis to apply those words to Jesus. The prophets were longing for the Promised Messiah and when they spoke about Him, they knew they were speaking about Him.

39 LXX for Deuteronomy 23:1 "Οὐκ εἰσελεύσεται θλαδίας καὶ ἀποκεκομμένος εἰς ἐκκλησίαν κυρίου"

The LORD God took upon himself the curse of the law when he died hanging from a tree. As a result, the curse of the law and effectively the law itself had come to an end so the prohibition on eunuchs entering the covenant community was removed and this eunuch could be welcomed and baptised.

The significance of this African follower of Jesus is hard to over-estimate. The power-house of Christian life and thought for the first 500 years was north Africa. Nearly all the major theologians were African, whether Origen, Tertullian or Augustine.

No sooner had Philip and the Ethiopian walked out of the water than Philip was whisked away by the Spirit to suddenly appear at Azotus (not very far away from Gaza). Philip, encouraged by what had happened, began preaching about Jesus along the coast all the way up to Caesarea.[40]

b. Saul of Tarsus (9:1-31)

The persecutions had been the wind spreading the fire of the Way of Jesus across Judea and Samaria, but a major boost to the international spread of Israel was about to happen. The twelfth apostle, of Jesus' choosing, was about to be revealed.

We know quite a lot about Saul of Tarsus (Paul was his Roman name), mostly because he shared so much about himself in all his letters. The Hebrew name Saul indicates that he was *desired* but his Roman name Paul simply means *small*.[41] He was of the tribe of Benjamin[42] and both his parents were Jewish. Both Paul and his father were Pharisees.[43] Tarsus was a Roman city and he was a free Roman citizen.[44] Though born in Tarsus he was brought up in Jerusalem[45] and he was tutored there under the eminent Gamaliel[46], which indicates that he was something of a high-flyer in legal and theological study. He had the trade skill of leatherworking or tent-making to pay the bills when his intellectual skills would not.[47]

---

40   It is interesting to note that this is the region that the ancient Philistines had occupied.

41   One ancient Christian writer said that Paul was just four and a half feet tall (150 centimetres).

42   Philippians 3:5

43   Acts 23:6. Paul may well have been one of Cilician zealots of Acts 6:9.

44   Acts 22:28

45   Acts 22:3

46   Acts 22:3

47   Acts 18:3

Paul was a man of intense passion and zeal, both before he followed Jesus and after. In Acts 9:1-2 we find him murderously chasing the scattering followers of the Way as they tried to escape his persecution in Jerusalem. Just as the Way was becoming international, so would the fierce opposition. Having obtained permission from the high priest to capture Jewish followers of Jesus, Paul headed for Damascus in Syria.

Paul himself told the story of what happened on his journey to Damascus many times in his letters and sermons.

Jesus appeared to him in brilliant light – "Saul, Saul, why do you persecute me?" (verse 4). It is wonderful that the union between Jesus and His followers is so close that harm done to them is harm done to Him. The Living God over heaven and earth is so identified with His church! (See also Matthew 25:40 and 45).

When Paul asked for the identity of the Lord, he is told – "I am Jesus, whom you are persecuting. Now get up and go into the city, and you will be told what you must do."

As we read later in one of Paul's descriptions of this event[48], the Lord had been prodding and goading Paul to this line of thinking for some time. Had Paul heard Jesus speak? Was he one of the Pharisees who had condemned Jesus to death? Somewhere along the line, Paul had been resisting something that was bothering him until this point.

Yet It must have been the psychological and religious equivalent of driving into a brick wall! In his religious zeal he had been attacking the very God he thought he was serving! From being a man of action, he became an incapacitated blind man who could not eat or drink anything for three days – verse 9. However, Jesus went ahead of Paul and arranged for a follower named Ananias to meet and heal Paul – verses 10-12.

Ananias couldn't believe what the Lord Jesus was commanding – verses 13-14. Surely someone like Paul could never change! Surely the power of the gospel could not stretch as far as a murdering, religious zealot! It must have been a terrifying thought for Ananias to voluntarily visit the man who was coming to Damascus to find and destroy the followers of Jesus.

---

48   Acts 26:14.

Jesus reply to Ananias is fascinating – "Go! This man is my chosen instrument to carry my name before the Gentiles and their kings and before the people of Israel. I will show him how much he must suffer for my name."

First, Paul was Jesus' choice of apostle to assist the international spread of His Name. The aspects of Paul that had been used for evil would be redeemed for good. Paul's passion, zeal and courage would be used to take the Name of Jesus to new territories and to proclaim this Name to the leaders of the age.

The same can be true for us. We may well have completely misused the abilities and opportunities that the Lord has given to us, yet even now the situation can be redeemed. How can we use these abilities and opportunities to lift up the Name of Jesus?

Second, Paul had brought persecution and suffering against the Way, but now he would be constantly on the receiving end. Jesus is always being persecuted by His enemies in every age and if we are to walk closely with Him then we too will share the fellowship of His sufferings. The path to spiritual maturity and fruitfulness is always the Way of the Cross.

Acts 9 :17 is such a wonderful verse. In spite of all of Ananias' fears, yet he completely trusted what Jesus told him and went straight to the given address and, while embracing him said "Brother Saul…" What a special moment that was for the history of Europe! Through Ananias the Holy Spirit filled Paul, healed him of his blindness, led him to be baptised and made him ready to eat some food. What a restoration! Saul had been so utterly humbled and physically crushed, yet now he was welcomed into the family of the Living God and restored physically, emotionally and spiritually! It is no surprise that the conversion of Saul was been perhaps the defining conversion story throughout all Christian history.

He immediately began to teach the truth of Jesus in the local synagogues – verse 20. His transformed life and teaching caused amazement – verses 21-22. Yet, his ability to demonstrate from the Old Testament Scriptures that Jesus really is the Divine Messiah rapidly grew.

In verse 23 we are told that he was based in Damascus for "many days". Given what Paul tells us in Galatians 1:11-18 this period lasted more than three years. In Galatians 1:11-12 he explains how he was instructed in the Way of Jesus not by any man but by Jesus Himself.

> ... I want you to know, brothers, that the gospel I preached is not something that man made up. *I did not receive it from any man, nor was I taught it; rather, I received it by revelation from Jesus Christ.*

Thus, we can understand why the Damascene Christians were so amazed by the phenomenal progress of Paul. But, where did this personal instruction from Jesus take place? Galatians 1:16-18.

> I did not consult any man, nor did I go up to Jerusalem to see those who were apostles before I was, but *I went immediately into Arabia*[49] *and later returned to Damascus. Then after three years, I went up to Jerusalem* to get acquainted with Peter and stayed with him fifteen days.

So, there was a truly amazing background to Acts 9:22, a background that enabled Paul to be called an apostle even though he did not meet the original requirements set out in Acts 1:21-22. As an apostle "born out of time" (1 Corinthians 15:8-9), Paul was given a special personal training by Jesus.

The same persecution that the other apostles experienced was soon turned against Paul as well – verse 23.

From being the star of the unbelieving Jews...
... he becomes their main enemy
From being wealthy and respected...
... he is reduced to escaping in a basket

There was something incredibly humiliating for the great Saul of Tarsus to be lowered down in a waste basket from Damascus as if he were a common criminal (verse 25). When Paul was listing all his most embarrassing weaknesses, he saves this episode as a sort of climactically bad moment – "In Damascus the governor under King Aretas had the city of the Damascenes guarded in order to arrest me. But I was lowered in a basket from a window in the wall and slipped through his hands" (2 Corinthians 11:32-33).

---

49 If we consider what Paul says about Mt Sinai in Galatians 4:25, it is likely that Paul was led by the Spirit to that Mountain of God to meet with Jesus (see Exodus 3:1-6).

He went up to Jerusalem, but as far as they were concerned he was still the Saul of Tarsus who was out to get them.[50] However, Barnabas (the Levite from Cyprus who sold his field in Acts 4:36-37) recognised that the new life of Jesus was genuinely at work in Paul – verse 27. He explained Paul's conversion experience (verse 27) and helped Paul to join the preaching team of Jerusalem (verse 28).

Paul's confrontational character was very evident, however (verses 28-30) and he provoked death threats from Gentile converts to Judaism. The passion of converts was meeting from opposite directions! The wiser apostolic leaders in Jerusalem realised that this was going to end badly and they returned him to his native Tarsus via the port of Caesarea. Paul needed to learn more lessons about being a wise as well as a bold and direct witness for Jesus. For the next few years Paul would learn those lessons in obscurity, making tents and leather goods in the marketplace of Tarsus.

> *There are those who ask why the Lord intervened directly in Saul's life and why he doesn't seem to do more of this to other people in the Bible or indeed today. However it is worth remembering that this was an unusual conversion of an unusual individual for a very unusual and very difficult task. Anyone who wishes for a similar conversion experience must also consider the opposition Paul was to face from this day onwards.*

With Paul out of the way, Luke tells us that the church in Jerusalem, Judea and Samaria enjoyed a time of peace and growth, full of the Spirit and full of the fear of the Lord – verse 31. This is a crucial moment in the Book of Acts. It is as if the initial stages in Jesus commission to the apostles had been completed.

In this peaceful atmosphere Peter decided to visit some of the newly formed churches. In Lydda he healed a paralysed man named Aeneas (9:32-35) and virtually everybody in the region began to follow Jesus too. The eye-witness testimony of Peter was authenticated by the fact that Peter was able to do the very things that Jesus had done. It was obvious that Jesus was alive and acting with power in His appointed apostles.

---

50   This fits well with the fact that he had spent much of the previous three years in Arabia learning from Jesus. He simply hadn't been part of the public Christian community for very long.

The people of Joppa asked Peter to come when a dearly loved Christian called Tabitha died. The fact that they no longer regarded death as the final word in the situation showed how deeply the resurrection of Jesus had gripped the hearts and minds of these believers. Peter came at their request and after prayer called Tabitha back to life.[51] Again this led to many people finding the new life of Jesus – verse 42.

The result of all this was that Peter no longer felt the need to go back to Jerusalem. As the churches spread out further and further, now Peter decided to live in Joppa with Simon the leather worker (verse 43).

c. Accepting the Gentiles (10:1-11:18)

With Peter moving out from Jerusalem, Jesus connected him to an enquirer called Cornelius. Cornelius was an Italian soldier, but he was searching diligently for the Living God, giving generously and praying regularly (verses 1-2). Jesus answered his search by sending an angel to direct Cornelius to Peter.

First, Jesus honoured the fact that Cornelius was doing the best he could as he searched for the truth. Cornelius knew that caring for the poor was the way of the Living God, so he started with what he knew. We often come across people in the same situation as we care for social need. There are all kinds of people getting involved with this work as they search for the truth. The example of Cornelius encourages us to reach out to them, taking their search seriously. Hebrews 11:6 – "anyone who comes to God must believe that He exists and that He rewards those who earnestly seek Him."

Second, receiving special visions and dreams is much more common around the world than we might realise. Many Muslim background believers were brought to Jesus through visions and dreams. Others have experienced the same. A dear friend called Elsie tells how she would be awakened in the middle of the night by Muslims who had been told of her address in a vision or dream. The way that Jesus dealt with Cornelius is still the way Jesus can deal with people today, especially with those who diligently seek him.

---

51   There is something reminiscent of Elijah about this miracle from Peter – 1 Kings 17:23-24. As Jesus points out in Luke 4:26, Elijah had ministered to a pagan woman, so now the servants of God were heading out to serve people who were further and further away from the old circle of Israel.

The issue of precisely where Cornelius stood on the road to full salvation is not made clear in this account and this is not the main point. It is the identity of Cornelius that is the key truth and his inclusion, not so much his conversion that is the point Luke wants us to understand. This is important because some want to make this incident a pattern for all individual conversions.

At another hour of prayer, the next day, Peter was very hungry and ordered some food (Acts 10:9-10). He was also given a vision and given that food was on his mind, the theme of the vision was preparing food!

Three times he was shown a big table cloth filled with all the different kinds of animals, clean and unclean, pigs as well as sheep, lizards as well as locusts. According to the Law of Moses (Leviticus 11) only the clean animals could be eaten and it would have been deeply offensive for Peter to even think about eating the unclean animals. No matter how hungry he was, a bacon sandwich was forbidden by the ancient Law.

However, on each occasion the LORD God Himself told Peter to eat all the animals. The LORD God Himself told Him to forget about the distinctions between clean and unclean! It is a shocking moment. We have already seen that forgiveness of sin was given through Jesus without any animal sacrifice, but now the full implications were becoming clear.

If the temporary law of Moses[52] had completed its purpose in preparing for the work of the Messiah, then the divisions between clean and unclean, Jew and Gentile had all disappeared.

It took time for Peter to think all this through – verse 17. Yet, when the Gentile messengers arrived inviting Peter to meet with a God-fearing Gentile who was looking for the truth (verses 19-23), he began to understand what the Lord was really teaching him. If all the animals were clean then all human beings were also clean, all in the same category before God.

In Leviticus there were three categories: holy, clean/common and unclean. All the non-Jewish nations of the world were classified as unclean along with pigs, predators, crabs, insects, death, disease and demons. Only clean

---

52   See Hebrews chapter 8 for a more detailed explanation of this.

people/property/animals could be brought into the holy presence of the LORD God. Therefore there was no way for a Gentile to meet the LORD God unless they first became a clean Jew.

Anything that was clean was acceptable within the assembly of Israel, within the church of God. Now that the Law of Moses had reached its fulfilment, the category of unclean had been abolished. The Lord returned to the time before Moses and Abraham when everybody in the world stood shoulder to shoulder in the same category. Abraham himself had been called when he was an uncircumcised pagan in ancient Babylon – (Joshua 24:2-3).

As understanding began to dawn, Peter went to Cornelius along with other believers from Joppa – verse 23. In Caesarea Cornelius was overjoyed to meet Peter – verses 24-25. The whole house was full of those who like Cornelius were anxious to find out how to achieve peace with the LORD God of Israel – verse 25.

In Peter's initial speech he indicates that he was already understood what Jesus was teaching in the vision – verses 27-29. By accepting this hospitality from Gentiles Peter had already walked across the barrier of the Law of Moses.

Cornelius explained about his own vision – verses 30-33 – and the Peter preached a magnificent sermon – verses 34-43. He begins by brilliantly summarising all the theological thinking that has been storming around his head for the previous 24 hours.

> *I now realise how true it is that God does not show favouritism but accepts men from every nation who fear him and do what is right.*

Peter then went onto explain all that had been happening. Jesus, the Jewish Messiah had come, appointed and authenticated by the LORD God (verses 36-38). The apostles were eye-witnesses of the fact that not only did the Jews reject their Divine Messiah with a Law-cursed death (verse 39), but that the Living God vindicated Jesus by raising Him from the dead (verse 40). Jesus had appointed these apostolic eye-witnesses of His genuine resurrection, people who had actually eaten meals with this Risen Messiah (verse 41). Then Jesus had commissioned them to tell everybody in the world that Jesus is the One who will judge every human being who ever lived – verse 42.

This should come as no surprise to anybody who knew the Hebrew Scriptures. The ancient prophets always said that anyone from any nation who believes in the Messiah would find a new life as their sins were forgiven[53] – verse 43.

Jesus had been thrust outside the Law by the Jewish people, so now He was available to everybody in the world without any of the distinctions and divisions contained within the Law.

This very reality was demonstrated while Peter was still speaking. The Jewish believers were used to the idea that Jewish people could be filled with the Spirit as they followed Jesus, but now they saw these foreigners being welcomed into Jesus' family, filled with the Spirit and praising God in all their 'pagan' languages (verses 44-45).

Peter saw all this and realised that if the Holy Spirit had welcomed them into the family of God then they needed to acknowledge them as members of Jesus' church as quickly as possible through baptism (verses 47-48).

Peter had received the personal guidance from Jesus, but the other Jewish believers had not so Peter had to return to Jerusalem to explain what had happened (11:1). They could hardly believe that Peter had accepted hospitality from the foreigners (verse 3), let alone baptised them into the church family.

Peter simply told them all what had happened (verses 4-17), concluding with the clinching argument – "if God gave them the same gift as he gave us, who believed in the Lord Jesus Christ, who was I to think that I could oppose God?"

> *Verse 15 is important because Peter explains that what happened to the Gentiles in Cornelius' house was identical to what had happened to the first disciples in chapter 2. This pouring out or filling or baptism of the Spirit was the very same, for Jew and for Gentile. The church was truly going global.*

All objections and hesitations disappeared (verse 18). In fact, they all began to praise the Lord God. All the ancient prophecies were coming true around them. People from all the nations of the world were being turned around and brought into the new life of Jesus the LORD.

---

53   For example, Genesis 12:3, Isaiah 19:19-25, Joel 2:28, Jonah etc.

Study 5   Bible Questions

Acts 9:1-31

1. Verses 1-2 – What state was Saul in at the beginning of this chapter? What was his intention and goal? How did he hope to achieve this? What would his thoughts have been concerning Jesus at this stage?

2. Verses 3-6 – What do Jesus' words to Saul say about what Saul was doing? Why did Jesus intervene with Saul at this time and in this place?

3. Verses 7-9 – Why didn't those travelling with Saul hear the voice of Jesus? Why was Saul blinded by this encounter? What might this have symbolised?

4. Verses 10-16 – What was Saul's initial intention when he met Ananias in Damascus? How would Ananias have been feeling about this? Why did Jesus want someone like Ananias to meet with Saul and speak to him?

5. Verses 17-19 – What do Ananias' actions say about his trust in Jesus? Why was it that Saul regained his sight at this point?

6. Verses 20-22 – What specifically did Saul begin to do and where? What sort of a response did he receive? Was this reasonable?

7. Verses 23-25 – Why were the Jews so intent on killing Saul at this stage? How would Saul have felt being treated like this compared to his previous way of life?

8. Verses 26-30 – What was the initial response of the believers to Saul's conversion? What does this say about the believers and their attitude to the gospel? What was their attitude towards him when he sought to leave? Why did Barnabas believe Saul? What effect did Barnabas have on Saul's life?

9. Verse 31 – Where has the church reached by this verse? Compare this to Jesus' instructions in Acts 1:8. What does this tell us? Why did the church enjoy a time of peace at this point?

10. Verses 1-31 – Why don't more people have a "Damascus Road" type experience? Why did Jesus select Saul for this conversion? Who do we know that we think is beyond the reach and power of the gospel? What does Jesus' encounter with Saul tell us about such people? What is our role in the meantime?

Study 5   Further Questions

Why were eunuchs excluded from the Old Testament church? What made it even more difficult for the eunuch in chapter 8 to be included as a full member of the church? Why was Cornelius previously excluded from the life of the church? How easy would it have been for a faithful Jewish Christian to accept people like this into their meetings? Which person or group of people do we feel are least likely to fit into our church meetings? Why? What should we do about it?

How could Jesus remove all the detailed laws concerning who and what is clean and unclean as easily as he did in his encounter with Peter in chapter 10? What does this tell us about these laws? What then should our attitude be to all of the laws prescribed in the book of Leviticus for example? Why?

Why did Cornelius and his household speak in different languages when they received the Holy Spirit in Acts 10:46? What does this tell us about this gift?

Study 5   Daily Readings

Day 1	Acts 8
Day 2	Acts 9
Day 3	Acts 10
Day 4	Acts 11:1-18
Day 5	Isaiah 53
Day 6	1 Kings 10:1-13
Day 7	Leviticus 11

The daily Bible readings are an opportunity to not only read through all of the material in the book under study, but also to read parts of the Bible that relate to the themes and issues that we have been considering. We try to make sure that we receive light from the whole Bible as we think through the key issues each week.

Children of the Revolution

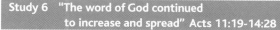

**Study 6   "The word of God continued
to increase and spread" Acts 11:19-14:28**

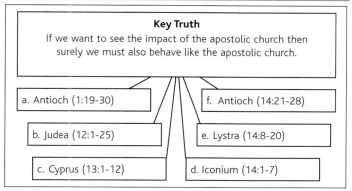

Key Truth
If we want to see the impact of the apostolic church then
surely we must also behave like the apostolic church.

a. Antioch (1:19-30)

f. Antioch (14:21-28)

b. Judea (12:1-25)

e. Lystra (14:8-20)

c. Cyprus (13:1-12)

d. Iconium (14:1-7)

a.   Antioch (1:19-30)

The persecution that began with the murder of Stephen in Acts 8:1 had scattered followers of Jesus out to Cyprus and up the coast to Antioch. This first wave shared the message of new life only with Jewish people, but then those Jews with a North African and Mediterranean background began to tell all the foreigners about Jesus too – verses 19-20. This was a very successful strategy – verse 21.

Although the leaders in Jerusalem had agreed with Peter about welcoming foreigners into God's family, yet they wanted Barnabas to encourage[54] what was happening at Antioch – verses 22-24. Full of the Spirit, Barnabas helped to bring many people into the Way of Jesus.

However, it must have quickly become clear that there was far too much for him to do alone. Barnabas remembered that very impressive if slightly confrontational man called Saul who they had sent away to Tarsus a few years earlier. He took a bit of finding (verse 25), but Saul had matured into a excellent church leader and for a whole year Saul was able to work as an apprentice to Barnabas (verse 26).

---

54   Given that he was 'the son of encouragement'.

The fascinating fact at the end of 11:26 is that the name "Christian" was first used at Antioch. The fact that this became the generic name for followers of Jesus is of great significance. Why weren't they called something like "Messiahians", retaining the Hebrew language? Already the centre of gravity was shifting to the international stage and the word to describe them was from an international language.

b. Judea (12:1-25)

A prophet named Agabus, from Jerusalem, correctly predicted a widespread famine that came in the time of Claudius. We learn in Acts 12:20 that the food supply for Judea was controlled by Herod. Therefore the international church family began to make special provision for the churches back in Judea. This was yet another powerful expression of the fact that Israel had become an international family with no national boundaries, full of people from every background, both Jews and Gentiles.

Herod was certainly an evil man, deeply opposed to the followers of Jesus. In Acts 12:1-2 he had one of the original disciples murdered in order to gain popularity with the unbelieving Jews. James, the brother of John, who had led the Jerusalem church was so callously killed. The partnership of those two brothers, the sons of thunder[55], who had argued about being on the right and left hand of Jesus, was over. John would go on for many more years, yet we can only imagine the grief this was to him.

Drunk with his notoriety, Herod aimed to repeat his evil with Peter. Arrested and imprisoned during the Feast of Unleavened Bread, like Jesus, Peter was to be given a public show trial after Passover. Put under the very strictest guard, escape was impossible from a human point of view (verses 3-4).

Yet, the church was praying.

Herod thought he was like a god on earth (12:21-23), but he received a warning that all his power was as nothing to the God of heaven. All his armed guards, chains and prison walls were no match for even one of the angelic host.

It is good to remember angels are more like warriors than babies, more like soldiers than fairies. This angel didn't bother with polite or gentle etiquette

---

55   Mark 3:17

but simply struck Peter and told him to get up (verse 7). With brisk orders, this warrior angel took Peter outside the prison, dispensing with chains, guards and gates as if they weren't there.

Peter, of course, thought he was dreaming and it wasn't until he was standing in the street outside, alone, that he realised what had happened (verse 11).

The church prayer meeting was happening in the house of Mary the mother of John Mark (the man who wrote the gospel of Mark and who was a temporary companion of Paul – see Acts 13:5 & 13). The servant girl came to answer the door and was so amazed that their prayers had been answered that she didn't even open the door. While the church continued to pray for Peter's release, Rhoda told them that he HAD been released... but they didn't believe her. They assumed that Peter's angel was trying to get in rather than Peter himself![56]

Eventually, by persistent knocking, Peter made the church realise that they could stop praying for his release and let him in. He left a message for the new leader of the Jerusalem church, James, the half-brother of Jesus, who wrote the book of James. By tradition he is referred to as James the Less.

How unbelieving our prayer meetings can be! Do we really expect our prayers to be answered? In the time of crisis many of the believers gathered for a night of desperate prayer (verse 12). When was the last time your own local church did this? Are the circumstances of these times not urgent enough to warrant a night of desperate prayer? Yet, when we pray together in this way, and find our unity deepened and our mission strengthened, we should expect that the Living God, who is more generous than the most indulgent parent, will certainly answer us.

When the church prays together in this way, things happen.

Herod did not discern this display of divine power and cruelly blamed it on the sixteen guards. Yet, his day of judgement was fast approaching (verses 19-23). Heading to the coast, Herod arranged a public audience with the people of Tyre and Sidon who desperately needed him to supply them with food.

---

56   It is remarkable that they were so comfortable with the idea that Peter's personal angel might be knocking on the door of the house. When we consider Jesus' teaching on the subject in Matthew 18:10, surely such a visitor would be worth allowing into the house!

Dressed in his finest clothes he delivered a public speech with such eloquence that people began to praise him as a divine figure. Herod actually believed this stupid praise and provoked a fierce response from the one true God over all creation (verse 23).

In spite of all Herod's opposition and boasting, the Way of Jesus continued to make progress – verse 24.

Having delivered aid for the famine, Barnabas and Saul returned to Antioch, taking John Mark with them (verse 25).

Paul's first missionary journey was about to begin.[57]

c. Cyprus (13:1-12)

Up to this point the centre of attention had been Jerusalem, but from this point on Antioch begins to take centre stage. Antioch, with Alexandria in North Africa, would become one of the centres of Mediterranean Christianity in the early centuries.

We can see something of the international Jesus revolution when we look at the leadership team described in Acts 13:1-3.

Barnabas was a Levite from Cyprus, a very gifted leader ready to travel as the need arose.

Simeon was called Niger which means that he was black, perhaps from the ancient Nigerian or Ethiopian empires.

Lucius was from Cyrene, which according to Acts 2:10 was part of North Africa near to Libya. Some have wondered whether he might be the Luke who wrote Jesus' biography and this current volume of Acts.

Manaen had been brought up with Herod the tetrarch. Herod was well connected with the Roman imperial family, so Manaen was clearly from a very influential and politically powerful background.

---

57 We should not forget that Luke is telling us only one aspect of the global expansion of Israel at this time. Other apostles and disciples had gone east, north and south of Jerusalem, taking this message to other nations and cultures. Thomas is said to have travelled down through Egypt and Ethiopia on his way to India. Others went into Syria and Persia. Book 2 of Eusebius' *Church History* is a useful starting point to discover this wider history. It is said that Jude and Bartholomew almost went to India and then on into China.

Saul, as we have seen, was a Roman citizen with a multi-cultural, multi-lingual background. In 1 Corinthians 14:18 he claims to speak more languages than the Corinthians. He was educated at the highest level and had been part of a violent fundamentalist group.

This diverse international collection of leaders, with their varied skin colours and cultures, must have been such a powerful statement of the kind of global family that Jesus was creating.

United together in worship and prayer the Holy Spirit indicated that Barnabas and Saul were the ones needed for the mission that was on His heart – verse 2.[58] How many churches would spare their very best leaders for an international mission lasting so many months?

This was an incredible moment for Mediterranean history. The first faltering steps had been taken as the family of Jesus had spread out from Jerusalem to Judea and Samaria. Now that it was established in Antioch a new dynamic vision had arrived. Instead of slowly being forced out by persecution, the Antiochene church was taking the initiative, sending out their best people to spread the message of new life in Jesus.

Are we like that? How are we taking the initiative in our area? What are we doing to put Jesus' new life on the agenda in our town or region? Are we supporting, employing, sending out workers who will show the Way of Jesus in word and action? Are we planting new churches? As I write, only a tiny percentage of modern Britain are genuinely following the Way of Jesus. Just as the Antiochene church were united in desperate prayer and fasting, that is obviously what we must do.

Nights of prayer, days of fasting, sharing all we have, caring for the needs of others and deeply studying the Scriptures – if we want to see the impact of the apostolic church then surely we must also behave like the apostolic church.

---

58   It is important to note the personality of the Holy Spirit. We must never refer to Him as an 'it'. He is a vibrant person who speaks, feels, acts and thinks. He is the member of the Trinity associated with personal fellowship (2 Corinthians 13:14). Like that church of Antioch we should be in such warm fellowship with Him that we too know what He is saying to us, how He is leading us. If we cannot recognise His voice, perhaps we need to walk more closely with Him – Galatians 5:16-26.

From the coastal port of Seleucia, they crossed to Cyprus. John Mark was with them (verse 5), though it may have been too early for him to be engaged in such a ground-breaking mission. They immediately established their typical pattern of the missionary journeys – explaining the Scriptures in the local synagogues (verse 5).

At Paphos the proconsul[59], Sergius Paulus, heard about the wonderful new life of Jesus and asked them to hear more of the Scriptures (verse 7). In Acts 9:15 Jesus had promised that Paul would tell rulers about Him, and this was the first of many such moments. However, a sorcerer from a Jewish background was part of the proconsul's staff and, for fairly obvious reasons, was very opposed to any serious study of the Scriptures.[60]

With the crossing of cultural barriers comes new cultural and spiritual conflicts. The Holy Spirit filled Paul (verse 9) and led him to confront the devilish schemes of Elymas, even making him temporarily blind (verse 11). His physical blindness was intended as a comment on his spiritual blindness.

The reaction of the proconsul is important. He could see that here was something much more substantial than the creepy world of the occult, yet what amazed him was "the teaching" about Jesus (verse 12). We must never forget this. No matter what miracles we may experience, no matter what social revolutions we may be involved with, what really changes the world is the teaching of Jesus – His birth, life, teaching, death, resurrection, ascension and return, not only from the four biographers and the apostles, but also from the ancient law and prophets.

Jesus Himself is the power behind all the world changing service and action.

From Cyprus they sailed on to Perga on the south coast of Asia Minor (modern day Turkey). The mission was too much for John Mark, who may have never travelled beyond Jerusalem until a year before, so he went back to his mother in Jerusalem – verse 13. Paul and Barnabas headed inland to the Antioch that was part of Psidia. Again they entered the synagogue and when asked, Paul explained the Scriptures (verses 14-16).

---

59   A proconsul administered the land belonging to a member of the Roman senate.

60   Leviticus 19:26; Deuteronomy 18:10-14; 2 Kings 17:17, 21:6.

The reading had been from the Law and the Prophets, so Paul explained how all that the Law and the Prophets spoke about was being fulfilled at that very time. His speech was designed to give a sense of the weight of history behind the global expansion of Israel, the church of the Living God.

Paul addressed his words not only to the Jews but also to the foreigners who had joined the synagogue. The ancient people of Israel had already been an international people from the very beginning, having stayed in Egypt for more than 400 years (verses 16-20). When this people settled in Canaan they wanted to be like the nations in a bad way, wanting a king just like all the other nations (verses 20-21). However, after that failed the LORD God gave them a king who was more like Himself, a king who was not only thinking and writing about the Messiah (see verses 32-37), but he was a key ancestor of the Messiah.

This Promised Messiah had now been born, the Saviour Jesus (verse 23). Even the greatest of all the prophets, John, who had so thoroughly challenged Israel to repent and get ready for the Messiah, declared that he was nothing compared to Jesus (verses 23-25).

History had reached its fulfilment.

> Brothers, children of Abraham, and you God-fearing Gentiles, it is to us that this message of salvation has been sent.

Paul directly challenged his hearers to understand the moment and respond in a better way than the religious leaders in Jerusalem had done.

Jesus is for everybody, whether Jew or foreigner, whether 'religious', pagan, agnostic or atheist.

Even when the Jerusalem people condemned Jesus to the cursed death of hanging from a tree, this was the fulfilment of history, prophesied long ago (verses 27-29). The Living God had all this in mind because He wanted to open up the Messiah's salvation to the whole world rather than confining it with the Jewish legal system. So, even though Jesus had been rejected by the Jews and the Law of Moses, yet He was resurrected – to a new life beyond those national divisions. For many days He proved the reality of His resurrection life to His appointed eye-witnesses (verses 29-30).

The resurrection of the Messiah was prophesied by both David and Isaiah.

Paul quotes from Psalm 2:7 but everybody in the synagogue would know the very next bit. Yes, the Messiah would be vindicated by His Father when the nations attacked and rejected Him, but the outcome of that would be the Messiah receiving an international inheritance encompassing the whole world.

> I will proclaim the decree of the LORD: He said to me, "You are my Son; today I have become your Father. *Ask of me, and I will make the nations your inheritance, the ends of the earth your possession.*

The quotation from Isaiah 55:3 also required his audience to know the next verses. The promises made to David were of an everlasting Kingdom – therefore there had to be an immortal, everlasting King, raised up beyond the power of death. But, the resurrected Davidic King would be for all the peoples, reaching out to all the nations.

> Give ear and come to me; hear me, that your soul may live. I will make an everlasting covenant with you, my faithful love promised to David. See, I have made him a witness to *the peoples*, a leader and commander *of the peoples*. Surely you will summon nations *you know not*, and *nations that do not know you* will hasten to you, because of the LORD your God, the Holy One of Israel, for he has endowed you with splendour. Seek the LORD while he may be found; call on him while he is near.

The third quotation, from Psalm 16:10, is the same point that Peter made in his Pentecost speech back in Acts 2. We know that the prophet David was speaking about Jesus rather than himself because David died and decayed away. However, Jesus died and was quickly resurrected (verses 35-37).

In the Law forgiveness of sin was tied into repeated animal sacrifices and these sacrifices could only be offered by ceremonially clean Jews giving the Gentiles no hope of salvation (unless they became Jews).

Now, however, Jesus death and resurrection has opened up forgiveness of sins to anybody and everybody, whether Jews or Gentiles. Anyone who trusts and follows Jesus will be accepted by the Living God, regardless of their background or nationality. Whereas the Law of Moses kept most people out of the picture, the Way of Jesus brings everybody into the picture (verses 38-39).[61]

Nevertheless, Paul quotes from Habbakuk 1:5. There is still the danger of rejecting and disbelieving the LORD God. The international world burst in on the people of Habakkuk's day in terrible judgement. All that they had trusted in was smashed away. Only those who rejoice in "God my Saviour" can handle all that the Living God is doing.

Paul's speech was a real blockbuster, and many people of both Jewish and international background wanted to know more (verses 42-43). It is interesting that Luke summarises Paul's message as "the grace of God" (verse 43). Even at this early stage Paul had such a passion for the free and gracious salvation in Jesus that cannot be earned by any human religion or effort. This message had such an impact that (verse 44) "on the next Sabbath almost the whole city gathered to hear the word of the Lord."

How exciting that must have been! Paul had shown the international character of the Way of Jesus and throughout the week it must have become the dominant topic of conversation throughout the whole city. Yet, those Jews who were the "scoffers" of verse 41 were jealous of the impact that Jesus was having rather than the impact their narrow rejection of the Messiah.

Paul and Barnabas were not intimidated by this abuse and again turned to the Scriptures. The Way of Jesus came first to the Jews, but in their rejection of Him it was opened up to the other nations as well. The prophet Isaiah prophesied that the people of Israel would reject the Divine Messiah and yet the LORD God would bring salvation to the ends of the earth (to use the very phrase that Jesus Himself used in Acts 1:8). So, again, in quoting Isaiah 49:6, Paul is assuming that his audience know the very next bit that prophesied that the nation of Israel would despise and abhor her Messiah.

---

61   The Law of Moses was prophesying all this, yet couldn't bring it about. The Law is a vast system prophesying and presenting the reality of Jesus the Messiah. It was a multimedia signpost pointing to the Promised Messiah. Yet, in order to fulfil the Law Jesus had to bring it to a conclusion.

(The LORD) says: "It is too small a thing for you to be my servant to restore the tribes of Jacob and bring back those of Israel I have kept. I will also make *you a light for the Gentiles, that you may bring my salvation to the ends of the earth."* This is what the LORD says — the Redeemer and Holy One of Israel — *to him who was despised and abhorred by the nation*, to the servant of rulers: "Kings will see you and rise up, princes will see and bow down, because of the LORD, who is faithful, the Holy One of Israel, who has chosen you."

However, although all the non-Jewish people in the area were thrilled at their invitation to join Jesus' kingdom, there were certain Jews who used their connections to stir up serious trouble for Paul and Barnabas, so much so that they apostles were thrown out — verse 50.

Following the commands of Jesus in Luke 9:5, they shook the dust off their shoes as a protest and moved on. Nevertheless the Jesus-followers they left behind were filled with the joy of the Spirit — verse 52.

d. Iconium (14:1-7)

The pattern that we see in Iconium seems to be the pattern that is repeated throughout the missionary journeys. We will see the following pattern time after time.

- They arrived and reasoned from the Scriptures in the local synagogue.
- Many Jews and Gentiles trusted Jesus and a local international church began to grow.
- The unbelieving Jews stirred up trouble.
- The apostles were forced to leave.

We are told that they stayed a long time in Iconium, despite (or perhaps because of) all the opposition — verse 3. The Scriptures were explained and their testimony was authenticated by the power of the Spirit in their actions. Opposition alone wouldn't stop them and only when they were about to be murdered did they make the short journey to Lystra — verses 4-6.

e. Lystra (14:8-20)

Luke shows us so many ways that Paul resembled Peter. Peter had healed a man crippled from birth in Acts 3 and now Paul does the same. Peter was miraculously rescued from prison in Acts 12 and so was Paul in Acts 16. Peter had a vision and so did Paul. Luke obviously had so many stories and incidents he could have selected, but he chose these so that we would see that the international work of Paul was in complete harmony with the work of Peter and those who remained in Jerusalem. Luke wants us to see that Paul was a true apostle just as Peter was.

Always ready to try something new, Paul seems to have begun his outdoor, public preaching in Lystra. Seeing the congenitally lame man listening in the crowd, Paul got slightly carried away and shouted "Stand up on your feet!" The man was healed and jumped up.

However, if we compare this to what Peter said in Acts 3:6 we can see why there was trouble in Lystra.

Peter had said – "In the Name of Jesus Christ of Nazareth, walk" whereas Paul simply said "stand up on your feet". In neglecting to mention the Name of Jesus, Paul made an error that quickly got out of control. The crowd forgot what Paul had been saying and focussed on the fact that an apparently ordinary human being had commanded a lame man to walk and his legs or feet had been fully formed and strengthened. Only the gods can do such things! They concluded that Paul and Barnabas had to be the Greco-Roman gods in human form.[62] This was the moment that the pagan priests had always dreamed of and (verse 13) raced to get the appropriate wreaths and sacrifices.

Paul and Barnabas were horrified and tearing their clothes in alarm they rushed into the crowd shouting a very challenging message – verses 15-18.

Paul and Barnabas were just ordinary men (verse 15) but the power they had seen healing the lame man was from the Living God who had good news for them. The Greco-Roman gods were not as old as the universe. They were ultimately players on a stage that they did not make. Paul and Barnabas had good news from the Living God who actually made not only the earth but

---

62   When you consider all the mythological stories about these 'gods' it is easy to see why the crowd drew this conclusion.

even the heavens (high above the 'gods'). This Living God has seen the way He has been ignored, the way that the nations have worshipped the things He made rather than Himself – verse 16. Nevertheless, He has provided constant testimonies to His reality. He has sent rain from the heavens that are high above the 'home of the gods' on Mt Olympus. High above the 'gods' He has maintained the seasons and He has provided all the food and enjoyment they have ever known – verse 17.

It was a powerful argument against the little pagan gods, but it was barely enough. The crowd was not happy about this, so it was easy for the unbelieving Jews from the previous two cities to stir up a revolt against the apostles. Within such a short time the apostles went from humans to gods to criminals! Dragged outside, Paul was very nearly killed and the new Christians had to care for Paul (or perhaps pray for his healing and restoration) till he was fit for travel the next day.

Popularity is not always a good thing. If we are forgotten and it is really Jesus who is popular then praise God. But if WE have become the centre of attention it will always end in total disaster.

f.   Antioch (14:21-28)

It was time to head back to the sending church of Antioch in Syria. Even as they passed through Derbe they had a wonderful time and "won a large number of dsciples" – verse 21. Passing back through the cities they had visited they were able to encourage the new churches.

The words of encouragement they left with the churches were not, perhaps, the first ones we might think of: "We must go through many hardships to enter the kingdom of God" – verse 22.

Actually, this was the best possible strength and encouragement. Perhaps these new Jesus-followers were worried about all the opposition, about the fasting and nights of prayer, about the self-denial and ridicule, about the beatings, imprisonments and even executions. Had it all gone wrong? Were they disobeying the LORD somehow? No! All these were glorious signs that they were on the right track, that they were genuinely following in the footsteps of the Crucified God, the Suffering Servant. The path to the glory of Jesus can only be through the sufferings of Jesus.

The apostles had not been able to organise these local churches on their first visit, so now they made sure they had some suitable leaders – verse 23.

So, they travelled back to Antioch in Syria, sailing from Attalia. When they arrived there must have been great excitement. How had it gone? How did all the pagan nations respond to the global family of God in Jesus the Messiah?

Paul and Barnabas gave a through report – verse 27. The Living God had indeed opened the door of His kingdom to all different nations of the world.

After this long and demanding mission, Paul and Barnabas spent a long time in the slightly calmer work in Antioch – verse 28.

Study 6   Bible Questions

Acts 14:1-20

1. Verses 1-2 – Why did Paul and Barnabas make it a habit to go first in to the Jewish synagogue? Why did the Jews who refused to accept the message become so hostile towards Paul and Barnabas? Why couldn't they just dismiss them as wrong and ignore them?

2. Verses 3-7 – What is Paul and Barnabas' response to the opposition they face? Why? How does the Lord respond to Paul and Barnabas' commitment? What part do signs and wonders play in the preaching of the gospel?

3. Verses 1-7 – In what way does the gospel unite Jews and Gentiles? What stops Paul and Barnabas from spreading the good news?

4. Verses 8-10 – On which other occasion was a crippled person healed in the book of Acts? Who carried out that healing and what did this person say? How are Paul's words here different?

5. Verses 11-13 – What is the response of the people to what Paul and Barnabas had done? Is this understandable? What does this tell us about the religious background of the people in this city?

6. Verses 14-18 – How do Paul and Barnabas react to the crowd's antics? How does Paul's speech here differ from his speech in chapter 13? Why is this?

7. Verses 19-20 – What had the crowd back in Iconium planned to do to Paul and Barnabas? What happened to Paul now? What does the fact that there were disciples in this city say about the result of Paul and Barnabas' speech? What did Paul do after the disciples gathered round him? Why?

8. Verses 1-20 – What indications are there about the existence of a church in Iconium and Lystra at the beginning of this chapter and at the end? What encouragement should this give us as we seek to tell people about Jesus?

Study 6   Further Questions

Why was it that in chapter 12, James was put to the sword and yet Peter was miraculously released from prison? Why on this occasion isn't Peter told to go back into the temple and proclaim the gospel as he was when he was released in chapter 4? What does all this tell us about the way the Lord deals with his people?

The church at Antioch fasted and prayed and then laid hands on Barnabas and Paul before they went out to do missionary work. Why? Paul and Barnabas then do the same thing to appoint leaders in 14:23. What effect do these actions have? Should we do the same today?

Why would Paul and Barnabas have told the young Christians that they "must" go through many hardships to enter the kingdom of heaven? What hardships are you currently going through? What will the outcome of your hardships be?

Study 6   Daily Readings

Day 1	Acts 11:19-30
Day 2	Acts 12
Day 3	Acts 13:1-12
Day 4	Acts 13:13-52
Day 5	Acts 14
Day 6	Isaiah 42
Day 7	Habakkuk 1

The daily Bible readings are an opportunity to not only read through all of the material in the book under study, but also to read parts of the Bible that relate to the themes and issues that we have been considering. We try to make sure that we receive light from the whole Bible as we think through the key issues each week.

The Unknown God

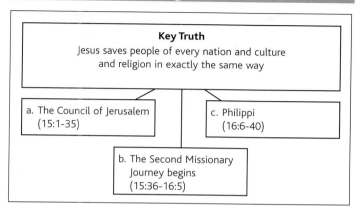

Key Truth

Jesus saves people of every nation and culture and religion in exactly the same way

a. The Council of Jerusalem (15:1-35)

c. Philippi (16:6-40)

b. The Second Missionary Journey begins (15:36-16:5)

a. The Council of Jerusalem (15:1-35)

In the light of all that had happened with all the non-Jewish people coming into the family of the LORD God if Israel, there was an urgent need for the global church leadership to gather together to set everything out in clear and simple terms.

The first great council of the global church was provoked when some Judeans tried to turn the clock back, as if Jesus the Messiah had not been born or died or been resurrected!

They went to Antioch to oppose the Way of Jesus with this teaching: "Unless you are circumcised according to the custom taught by Moses you cannot be saved." – verse 1.

This verse helpfully summarises the great theological controversy of the first century. As we read through the New Testament books we find this same issue confronting us time after time. Luke so helpfully distils the argument down to this simple statement, so that we can always refer back to this statement if we want to know what all the fuss is about in the apostolic letters.

As we have seen, the Law of Moses divided the world into clean and unclean. The ceremonially clean Jews were able to come into the church (assembly) of the Living God whereas all the other nations had to stay outside – with the pigs, dogs, demons, diseased and dead.

In fact, this division between Jews and Gentiles goes back even earlier than Moses to the time of Abraham. In Genesis 17 Abraham received a Law that required all males in every generation to be circumcised if they were going to be part of the covenant blessings of the LORD God. The uncircumcised male had to be cut off from the family of God – Genesis 17:14.[63] Foreigners who joined the people of God had to be circumcised before they were welcomed in – Genesis 17:12.

Throughout the book of Acts we have seen the apostles explain that Jesus the Messiah was rejected by those who claimed to be keeping the law. His death demonstrated this rejection, showing him to be cursed. Yet his death under the Law signifies the end or the fulfilment of the law, as Paul argues in Romans 7:1-6. The old distinctions no longer have any meaning.[64] Everybody, whether pagan or Jew, whatever their state of circumcision, stood shoulder to shoulder in the same camp, all needing the same forgiveness and new life that the Risen LORD Jesus offered.

Circumcision or uncircumcision made no difference one way or the other.[65] The only requirement for forgiveness and new life was following Jesus. Without getting over any hurdles whatsoever, anybody and everybody could simply call upon Jesus and be taken on as His disciples, given a righteous and Spirit-filled life with the Living God for free.

The Way of Jesus is free – cost free for us; free from religion; free from division.

---

63 The play on words is significant. In the Hebrew Scriptures a covenant is 'cut'. The 'cut' covenant was signified by the cutting of circumcision. Those that refused the cut in their flesh would be cut off from the covenant.

64 Throughout the Book of Acts we have seen the apostles explain that because Jesus the Messiah was rejected by the circumcised people of the Law and because He Himself was rejected by the Law in His death, then the old divisions of circumcision/uncircumcision or Jew/Gentile had no meaning anymore.

65 As Paul writes in Galatians 6:15, it makes no difference to a person's salvation whether a person is circumcised or not.

These Judeans in Acts 15:1 were arguing that the real sign of being right with God was circumcision. They saw these ancient laws as being the real thing and Jesus had to fit in with them… rather than the other way around. Yes, it was tempting to avoid the trouble that Paul and Barnabas had experienced by pretending that Jesus was not the full answer, that He was only useful if He could be accommodated within the religion of Law and circumcision. To the 'Judeans' Jesus' life, death, resurrection and ascension were not sufficient on their own, but they needed to be seen within and alongside the requirements of the Law. However, that would be a terrible perversion that would have destroyed the international family of the Living God at the very beginning. Paul's passionate words at the end of his letter to the Galatians make this so clear:

> Those who want to make a good impression outwardly are trying to compel you to be circumcised. The only reason they do this is to avoid being persecuted for the cross of Christ. Not even those who are circumcised obey the law, yet they want you to be circumcised that they may boast about your flesh. May I never boast except in the cross of our Lord Jesus Christ, through which the world has been crucified to me, and I to the world. Neither circumcision nor uncircumcision means anything; what counts is a new creation. (Galatians 6:12-15)

In Acts 15:2 Barnabas and Paul immediately recognised the terrible danger and sharply opposed the racist religious Judeans. Being so far removed geographically and in time from this debate may leave us feeling that it is rather irrelevant. However, the importance of opposing this error ought to be understood in the context of the breaking down of the barrier between Israel and the rest of the world. This is what has dominated our thinking throughout Acts so far, yet here, an issue arises that seeks to reverse this work. This needed to be properly addressed so Paul and Barnabas led a group up to Jerusalem to meet with the global leadership – verse 2.

On the way they shared reports of how so many pagans were being welcomed into God's family as they followed Jesus. This news was very well received and they got the same warm reception when they got to Jerusalem – verses 3-4.

However, as they gave a full report some of the 'believers' who had not resigned their membership of the Pharisee party of Law-fanatics tried to enforce the obsolete ideas of circumcision and religious barriers – verse 5. As far as they were concerned, Jesus had changed nothing: outsiders still had to become Jews if they were going to join God's family.

The global leadership of the Way of Jesus considered this carefully – verse 6. How could they tolerate such a fundamental rejection of the death and resurrection of Jesus? How could they explain to these Pharisees that Jesus had taken Israel beyond their legal categories?

Peter took a lead in the matter reminding them all of what had happened with Cornelius and his whole household. The Holy Spirit had clearly welcomed them into God's family without any of them being circumcised – verse 8. They had been made clean by trusting Jesus NOT by conforming to the law of Moses or being circumcised – verse 9.

If the cleansing power of Jesus alone was good enough for the Living God, then why wasn't it good enough for mere human beings? Viewed as a way of salvation the Law was a heavy burden that had never delivered the glorious reality that Jesus Himself had done[66] – verse 10.

No! said Peter. Whether Jew or pagan, whether circumcised or not, everyone is saved the same way – through the wonderful and sufficient and unconditional grace of the LORD Jesus -verse 11.

Peter had stated the matter so well that everyone was completely silent as Paul and Barnabas gave a full report of how so many foreigners had been welcomed into God's family as they travelled around Asia Minor – verse 12.

When James, the half-brother of Jesus, spoke he drew the whole matter to a conclusion – verses 13-21. He noted that the Living God had already decided the matter by taking the Gentile people as His own people – verse 14. Quoting Amos chapter 9 was one of the most radical of all the relevant

---

66   The purpose of the Law had never been anything more than testifying to the reality of Jesus. If people had ever tried to use the Law to get right with God then it became a pointless, heavy burden. However, when it was seen as a signpost or presentation of the future work of the Messiah, then it had such a different feel. See Psalm 51:16-19 or Galatians 3:24-25.

prophecies. Amos saw the Lord God standing by the altar pronouncing terrible judgement against Israel (Amos 9:1ff). Israel will no longer be seen as any different from all the other nations (Amos 9:7) — all judged the same:

> "Are not you Israelites the same to me as the Cushites?" declares the LORD. "Did I not bring Israel up from Egypt, the Philistines from Caphtor and the Arameans from Kir?"

The LORD has been caring for all the surrounding nations just as He has for Israel. Yet, in destroying Israel the LORD would create a new international future for Israel, a future where all these different nations will gather in the tent of Israel.

> In that day I will restore David's fallen tent. I will repair its broken places, restore its ruins, and build it as it used to be, so that they may possess the remnant of Edom and *all the nations that bear my name*," declares the LORD, who will do these things. (Amos 9:11-12)

Therefore, James concluded, the leaders of the international Israel should not place artificial barriers in the way of these foreigners who have already received the Name of the LORD.

As a footnote to this critical decision, James suggests three things from the Law that the Gentiles would find helpful in God's family, three things that most of them would have heard about anyway given that the Law of Moses was so well known in so many countries across the world (verse 21).

As verse 29 says, the pagan background believers would do well to avoid anything to do with idol worship, sexual immorality and drinking blood. Giving this advice from the Law of Moses was not in any way insisting that the Gentiles had to become Jews! This is helpful advice from the Law for all Christians regardless of their religious or national background.

1. **Abstain from food polluted by idols.** Obviously, there was nothing intrinsically wrong with this, but so many of the new believers from pagan backgrounds would have found it very difficult to have any dealings with the pagan religions they had turned away from. In 1 Corinthians 8 and Romans 14 the apostle Paul explains all the thinking behind this.

2. **Abstain from sexual immorality.** Although Jesus also deals with this matter, yet the Law of Moses would be helpful to the new believers in understanding all the different aspects of sexual purity required in the kingdom of God. Even though the citizens of God's kingdom are not under this Law, yet precisely because the Law was such a wonderful signpost pointing to the reality of Jesus the Christian can learn so much from studying the Law.

3. **Abstain from blood.** This command is more complicated because it goes back to a time before the Law was given. After the Flood, Noah was given permission to eat meat yet eating blood was expressly forbidden – Genesis 9:4. Noah is the father of all humanity so this is a matter that concerns Jew and Gentile alike. This prohibition was reinforced in the Law of Moses (Leviticus 17:10-14).

Why is the eating of blood condemned so universally throughout the whole Bible? The explanation given in Leviticus 17:10-14 is that the life is in the blood and the blood is given to make atonement. For this reason, there is an incredibly profound respect for blood in the Bible. Some have suggested that the only blood that we should ever take is the blood of Jesus, because His is the only life that we should ever share. His life was given to make atonement for us and to eat animal blood undermines our respect for His blood.

Of course, all meat has some blood in it. However, normally the blood is largely drained out of the meat before we eat it. What about those dishes that are specifically and deliberately made with blood, like black puddings? Speaking as a man from Lancashire in the UK, where black puddings are widely eaten, this is by no means a theoretical question. If we take this passage seriously, then any meal where the intention is to consume blood (rather than meat) is not appropriate for the follower of Jesus.[67]

So, two men were chosen to return to Antioch with the letter, ensuring that everybody understood that the foreigners needed to be welcomed into the international family of God without any hurdles of circumcision or law.

---

67   A steak may have some blood left in it, but the intention is not to consume blood but to eat the meat. A black pudding is made with blood and the intention behind that dish is to consume blood. This is why Acts 15:20 forbids strangled animals. A strangled animal is killed with all the blood remaining in it. The intention of eating such an animal is to consume its blood.

Jude Barsabas (probably the brother of the Joseph Barsabas mentioned in Acts 1:23) and Silas (soon to be travelling companion of Paul) were chosen to verbally confirm the letter- verse 22 and verse 27. Both of these men were recognised preachers capable of encouraging and reinforcing the message – verse 32.

It was vitally important that the international churches knew that nobody had to become a Jew in order to be saved. Jesus saves Jews and Gentiles alike by His own grace and power. Jesus needs no assistance from the Law of Moses! The reality had come and the signposts were not longer required.

The letter was addressed not only to the church at Antioch but also to the Gentile Christians throughout Syria and Cilicia (the south eastern portion of Asia Minor).

The letter begins with a very important fact – "We have heard that some went out from us without our authorisation and disturbed you, troubling your minds by what they said" (verse 24). In modern times some have claimed that the leadership in Jerusalem was opposed to the inclusion of foreigners and sent people to fight against Paul. This is explicitly rejected here. The trouble makers were not sent by the church leaders in Jerusalem.

The letter and the visiting preachers were very well received and everybody was deeply encouraged – verses 30-34. It is a key sign of the developing church in Antioch that so many others had join the preaching and teaching team – verse 35.

b. The Second Missionary Journey begins (15:36-16:5)

With such a strong endorsement by the global church that all the nations needed to be welcomed into the international family of Israel, it was not long before Paul and Barnabas decided they ought to check on the progress of their recent converts.

However, it began with a disagreement. There is great encouragement in seeing the weaknesses and humanity of the apostles, especially the apostle Paul. When we see how much these servants accomplished for Jesus it can sometimes seem that they were super-human, lifted beyond the normal sinful struggles that the rest of us face each day. The Holy Spirit made sure that we saw the whole picture as He inspired Luke to write this history. He wanted us to see that with Paul's fierce passion and zeal was also an intolerance and impatience which needed many years to be rooted out. Maturity doesn't happen overnight: it takes years of suffering service.

We have already seen how Mark bailed out of the first missionary journey after Cyprus and returned to his mum in Jerusalem – Acts 13:13 & Acts 12:12. As far as Paul was concerned John Mark was damaged goods and should not be given a second chance. He needed people with his iron will and determination. He couldn't deal with someone who might run back to his mum when the going got tough.

Barnabas very sharply disagreed with Paul's attitude and judgement – verses 37-38. Barnabas was a more mature believer and his great strength was encouragement (Acts 4:36; 11:23).[68] He could see that Mark was going to be a wonderful servant of Jesus. The fact that Mark had pulled himself together and gone back to Antioch from Jerusalem was a very important sign of Mark's character. Furthermore, with hindsight, we can see that Barnabas was very wise in his judgement. Mark wrote one of the canonical biographies of Jesus – the Gospel of Mark. Furthermore, church history records how Barnabas and Mark continued their journey beyond Cyprus (Acts 15:39) and went onto Alexandria in North Africa. It is said that Mark founded the church of Alexandria, which with Antioch, became the second great pillar of Gentile Christian theology throughout the Mediterranean world for centuries.[69]

In later years Paul himself came to see the quality of Mark. 2 Timothy 4:11 – "Get Mark and bring him with you, because he is helpful to me in my ministry."

Paul took the Jerusalem preacher Silas and travelled north through Syria and into the south eastern portion of Asia Minor. They visited the local communities of Jesus followers, presumably encouraging them with news of the Jerusalem letter – verse 41.

---

68   Barnabas had given Paul a second chance. The Jerusalem apostles had sent him away to stay low in Tarsus (Acts 9:30) but Barnabas went to find him when there was an opportunity for service in Antioch (Acts 11:25).

69   The Jewish writer Philo seems to record the appearance of Mark's Alexandrian church in his book about the *Therapeutae*. He records how a new group had arisen in Alexandria, organised by bishops and deacons, and people needing the healing of their souls would find healing with them. By tradition Philo met with Mark who took him to see Peter and Philo became a follower of the Messiah he had longed for and studied for so long.

Via this overland route, Paul and Silas arrived back at the churches from the first missionary journey in Derbe and Lystra. Here they found a young man called Timothy who was highly recommended by the local churches (verse 2). Timothy's family background was a great symbol of the new chapter in Israel's history – his mother was Jewish and his father was Gentile (verse 1).

Knowing that they were going to be visiting many synagogues and speaking to so many Jews in the area, Paul wanted to remove any cultural obstacles that might have prevented them from listening to the Way of Jesus. Therefore, Paul circumcised Timothy. This might seem bizarre given the strong debates and arguments of Antioch in Acts 15:1-2. However, it shows how deeply Paul understood the issues. For purely cultural reasons, Paul would do whatever he could so that people would hear the good news of Jesus. If he needed to be a vegetarian or teetotal then he would do that so that no cultural obstacles got in the way. If circumcising Timothy would open doors to a Jewish audience, then Timothy needed to be circumcised.[70] If we are dealing with alcoholics then we might need to refrain from alcohol to reach them. If we are dealing with Hindus we refrain from beef, if Muslims we refrain from pork and learn all the other cultural signs that will help us to remove merely cultural obstacles from our witness to Jesus.

> 1 Corinthians 9:19-22 – "Though I am free and belong to no man, I make myself a slave to everyone, to win as many as possible. To the Jews I became like a Jew, to win the Jews. To those under the law I became like one under the law (though I myself am not under the law), so as to win those under the law. To those not having the law I became like one not having the law (though I am not free from God's law but am under Christ's law), so as to win those not having the law. To the weak I became weak, to win the weak. I have become all things to all men so that by all possible means I might save some."

However, as soon as people mixed any of these things with the gospel itself, then Paul had to take a strong stand. If people say that we MUST be circumcised *in order to be saved*, then we must all refuse to be circumcised so that the power and glory of Jesus is not undermined. If people say that we

---

70   As Paul writes in Galatians 6:15, it makes no difference to a person's salvation whether a person is circumcised or not.

MUST be teetotal or vegetarian or members of one specific church group in order to be saved then we should drink some wine and eat some meat and join other groups in order to keep the gospel free from these dangerous additions and deviations.

c. Philippi (16:6-40)

Paul was always keen to move into new areas, places where the news of Jesus had never yet been heard.[71] Paul, Silas and Timothy moved through central Asia Minor, but when they tried to swing north into Bithynia along the Black Sea coast "the Spirit of Jesus would not allow them to" (verse 7). Whether they had a vision, heard a voice or simply that the circumstances prevented them, they knew that the Spirit of Jesus had prevented them heading back east. It is worth reflecting on the way the Spirit guides and leads his servants in this work. From the outside, it is difficult to imagine what could be wrong with telling the gospel anywhere, yet the Living God has a perfect plan and a timetable and only through prayer will we receive this guidance in our evangelism.

They went west to Troas, to the region famous for the legendary battle of Troy. It could be argued that the ancient history of Europe was determined by the Battle of Troy, and yet another moment of great significance for European history was about to happen.

Paul had a dream about a European man begging for help – verse 9. Was it a real person who Paul later met? Was it perhaps Jason from Thessalonica (Acts 17:5-9)? Was it a symbolic figure representing the whole region... or even representing the European continent? Was it an angel pleading for the continent or region?[72] Whatever the case, Paul got the message and set out to cross, via the island of Samothrace, to the fishing centre of Neapolis.

It is important to note that in this section of the Book of Acts it is about 'we' rather than 'they' indicating that Luke had joined the apostolic party.

---

71   Romans 15:20 – "It has always been my ambition to preach the gospel where Christ was not known, so that I would not be building on someone else's foundation."

72   See Daniel 10:20 for the idea that Greece had an angelic angel. However it is not clear that these national princes are all that helpful!

Pushing straight on from Neapolis, they went inland to Philippi (verse 12). Philippi was a Roman colony and obviously took great pride and care about this privileged Roman status – as becomes clear in the events of Paul's stay and his letter to the young Philippian church.[73]

They spent a few days getting to know the place and because there probably was no synagogue, on the Sabbath they went down to the river to find a quiet place to pray. Some local business women had gathered there who drew Paul, Silas and Timothy into conversation – verse 13. A specialist in the rare and expensive purple cloth was visiting from Thyatira (a city back in Asia Minor). She was called Lydia and had been searching for the Living God – verse 14. Jesus opened her heart to reality and her whole household became followers of Jesus. Lydia had owned property in Philippi and she insisted that the apostolic party use her house as the base for the new Philippian church – verse 15. Lydia demonstrated that she had been given spiritual gifts by showing the gift of hospitality to Paul and his companions.

One day when they were going back down to the river to pray, another woman intercepted them, but this time it was a slave girl possessed by some kind of spirit (verses 16-18). This strange spirit gave her the ability to predict the future to a certain extent [74] but the spirit also recognised the spiritual reality that had invaded Philippi in the form of the apostles – "These men are servants of the Most High God, who are telling you the way to be saved."

The apostles certainly did not want this kind of recognition and yet she carried this on day after day, until finally Paul, in the Name of Jesus, commanded the spirit to leave the girl.

It is vital to note that Paul did not look for confrontation with spirits. He knew that this slave girl was not only a slave to humans but also to a spirit, yet he did not charge in like some kind of ancient 'ghost buster'. Jesus warned that simply driving out demons makes the situation worse if the person is not following Jesus – Luke 11:21-26. The apostolic way is to get on with the real

---

73   The letter to the Philippians revolves around the fact that followers of Jesus are citizens of His heavenly kingdom rather than citizens of any earthly kingdom. See the Book by Book Study Guide for more details.

74   It is important to realise the real but limited power that the occult world has. Just as the ancient magicians in Moses' day were able to do limited wonders, so too there was some genuine predictive power behind this slave girl. Behind all the con-men and tricksters, there are those with dark power.

business of sharing the Way of Jesus in words and actions. This is how the spiritual forces are driven out and the spiritual strongholds torn down. The spiritual stronghold of greed is torn down when people begin to follow Jesus' way of generosity and simplicity. The spiritual stronghold of lust is broken down when people follow Jesus into His life of purity and self-sacrifice. Driving out spirits must be done only after prayer and fasting and only as a final resort.[75]

Nobody minds what kind of 'spiritual' and 'religious' ideas people want to spread as long as they have no practical effect. As long as the 'gospel' is just about some far away land in the sky or some distant future then it makes no difference to anybody right here and now. However, when finances are affected then it cannot be ignored.

The owners of the slave girl arrest Paul and Silas on a fascinating charge – (verses 20-21) – "These men are Jews, and are throwing our city into an uproar by advocating customs unlawful for us Romans to accept or practise." In this accusation we see the psychology of the city. They wanted to make sure that their lifestyle and values were completely in line with the Roman empire. That was what they most valued and they did not dare to change that. The whole crowd felt the same way – verse 22 – and made sure they were severely beaten. Remember that Paul and Silas had received no trial and no opportunity to defend themselves. On the basis of a fabricated accusation they were "severely flogged" and imprisoned.

As Jesus taught (Luke 6:22-23) Paul and Silas were full of joy that they had been considered worthy of suffering for Jesus. They were praying and singing hymns, using the opportunity to witness to their fellow prisoners.[76]

Suddenly a strange earthquake shook the prison, having the curious effect of opening all the doors and breaking all the chains! The jailor, assuming that the prisoners had all run away, was about to kill himself. Yet, incredibly, Paul and Silas had (presumably) led the other prisoners to follow Jesus... and they were all still waiting patiently inside the prison!

---

75   Mark 9:17-29

76   Clearly a body of Christian hymns had already been written. In less than 20 years the great Christian musical tradition was well under way. Every generation of Jesus followers all around the world produce the musicians and hymn writers that express the praise and worship of each age.

The jailor was amazed[77] and realised that these prisoners had the answers to life, death and eternity – "sirs, what must I do to be saved?" The apostolic reply is so memorable: "Believe in the LORD Jesus, and you will be saved – you and your household." The human religions of the world require so much effort, so many rituals and rites, so many priests and experts, so many pilgrimages and sacrifices, so many chants and meditations. Here, bursting apart the flimsy tyranny of human religion, is the Way, Truth and Life of Jesus of Nazareth – the Eternal Word of the Father. He calls to each one of us to simply trust Him, follow Him, obey Him. At no cost to ourselves, as an unconditionally free gift, Jesus will take anybody and everybody as His disciples, as citizens in His kingdom.

That very night the jailor and his whole family were baptised as followers of Jesus. In a single night they passed over from death to life, from darkness to light, from hell to heaven. Straightaway they began to live out the new way of sharing all they had – verse 34. Now their food, house and resources were all to be shared with their new extended family just as we saw in Acts 2:42-47; 4:32-37.[78]

In the cold light of the day the city magistrates realised that they had no cause to keep the apostles in prison, so ordered their release – verses 35-36.

However, in a moment that would be the envy of any great novel writer or film maker, Paul reveals that he is a Roman citizen and will not be quietly disposed of. We can only imagine the colour draining out of the city officials as they released what they had done. They respected and feared the Roman Empire above all else, and now they had effectively declared war on Rome! The Roman Empire might come and destroy them for this offence – verses 38-39.

Why did Paul insist on this public apology? The future legal status of the Christian churches was at stake. If they were labelled as anti-Roman trouble makers then it would be disastrous for the spread of the Way around the Mediterranean. Paul had to make sure that the false accusations were retracted and an apology given, not for his own sake, but

---

77   In Acts 12:19 we saw what happened to guards who let prisoners escape.

78   According to Genesis 17:9-14 a household includes children as young as 8 days old. Therefore we should not limit the age or number of the people baptised: whether 8 day old baby or a 80 year old grandparent, the whole family were baptised into the family of Jesus.

for the sake of the Philippian church and the other churches in the region. Citizenship was an important issue and as Paul wrote later to the church he had established in this city, the citizenship that really mattered was of heaven (Philippians 3:20.)[79]

Before leaving they went to encourage Lydia's house church – verse 40.

---

79   See the Book by Book study guide on Philippians for more on this.

Study 7   Bible Questions

Acts 16:11-40

1. Verses 11-12 – According to these verses, how did Paul seem to plan his journeys?

2. Verses 13-15 – What was unusual about Paul's actions by the river? Who was at work in the life of Lydia? How did she demonstrate her new life?

3. Verses 16-18 – Who or what power was at work in the slave girl? What must her life have been like? Why did the spirit within the girl speak the truth about Paul and his message?

4. Verses 19-21 – How much truth was there in the allegation made against Paul and Silas? What motivated the owners of the slave girl in their attack on them?

5. Verses 22-24 – On what grounds did Paul and Silas receive a beating? What condition would they have been in following this treatment? How useful were Paul and Silas now, having been flogged and locked in prison?

6. Verses 25-26 – What were Paul and Silas doing during the night and why? How did God respond to their action? Who else heard what was going on?

7. Verses 27-30 – Why does the jailor consider killing himself? What is his response to Paul and Silas? Why hadn't the other prisoners escaped?

8. Verses 31-34 – How does the jailor demonstrate his new life? In what ways had he been saved?

9. Verses 35-40 – Why was Paul so insistent on a public exit from the city? Why did the officers agree to such action? How would the new group of believers in Philippi have felt seeing all this happen?

10. Verses 11-40 – Describe the life changes that happened in Philippi? What brought about such changes? Do you know anyone like Lydia, or like the slave girl or like the jailor? What can you do for them?

Study 7   Further Questions

Why was circumcision specifically the issue that often caused so much division? Is there a modern day equivalent issue that brings churches and believers into sharp dispute? What should be done if such a dispute does occur?

Should Christians today eat black pudding? Should Christians today eat only kosher or halal meat? Why? Can we dismiss all of the prohibitions of the council at Jerusalem, some of them or none of them?

Why would the Holy Spirit of Jesus prevent Paul and his companions from entering Asia or Bithynia to spread the gospel there?

Study 7   Daily Readings

Day 1	Acts 15
Day 2	Acts 16
Day 3	Genesis 17
Day 4	Amos 9
Day 5	1 Corinthians 9
Day 6	Galatians 2
Day 7	Philippians 1

The daily Bible readings are an opportunity to not only read through all of the material in the book under study, but also to read parts of the Bible that relate to the themes and issues that we have been considering. We try to make sure that we receive light from the whole Bible as we think through the key issues each week.

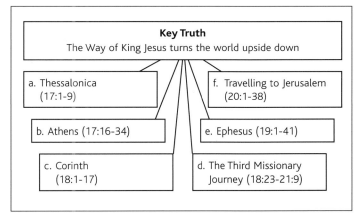

Key Truth
The Way of King Jesus turns the world upside down

a. Thessalonica (17:1-9)

f. Travelling to Jerusalem (20:1-38)

b. Athens (17:16-34)

e. Ephesus (19:1-41)

c. Corinth (18:1-17)

d. The Third Missionary Journey (18:23-21:9)

a.   Thessalonica (17:1-9)

It took great love, courage and confidence in Jesus to go so far outside their comfortable situations to share Jesus' new life with all the nations. They were travelling to new cities, new cultures. This sort of thing hadn't been done before. They had no "specialist training". There were no mission training colleges. In fact, there were no mission agencies of any kind. It was as simple as three followers of Jesus heading out with nothing more than a great love for humanity, a greater love for Jesus and hearts full of the Spirit.

Journeying on from Philippi, they passed through Amphipolis and Apollonia on to Thessalonica where there was a synagogue.[80] The fact that they had to travel through two cities in order to eventually find a synagogue tells us a great deal about the new challenges they faced after crossing into this new continent. Obviously the Law of Moses was far less influential in Europe than in Asia Minor.

In Thessalonica, Paul and Silas spent three weeks reasoning from the Scriptures in the synagogue. Each week they showed how the Law and the Prophets spoke

---

80   Each of these cities was about 30 miles journey apart: Philippi to Amphipolis, Amphipolis to Apollonia, and Apollonia to Thessalonica. Using horses, was it a hard day's journey between each city?

about Jesus, that He had to suffer before His resurrection.[81] We can speculate about all the different parts of the Hebrew Scriptures that they may have explained, but there are just too many possibilities to even begin to list.[82] Yet as we read the letter Paul writes back to the church here a short time later, we can see that Paul had explained so much about these truths that his letter only served as a reminder. (See for example 1 Thessalonians 4:1, 5:1-2).

Many Jews and internationals were persuaded and began to follow Jesus – verse 4.

However, the same pattern we have seen before happened again. Unbelieving Jews did not like the fact that Paul's explanation of the Hebrew Scriptures was winning so much popularity – verse 5. They rounded up local thugs, started a riot and went round to the house of the local synagogue leader, Jason. Jason had become a follower of Jesus, so he and other Christians in his house were beaten up while the mob looked for Paul and Silas. The accusation brought before the local officials was fascinating:

> "These who have turned the world upside down have come here too. Jason has harboured them, and these are all acting contrary to the decrees of Caesar, saying there is another king – Jesus" (New King James Version, verses 6-7).

Notice again how the accusation pivots on the social and political impact of the Way of Jesus. Their view of the world was one in which Caesar was on top

---

81   Cf 1 Peter 1:10-12

82   The way the whole creation happened through the Word of God – Genesis 1. The Voice of the LORD who walked in the Garden and promised His own human birth – Genesis 3. The promise of a seed of Abraham who would bless all the nations of the world – Genesis 12 and 15. The Word of the LORD who met Abraham and signed the both sides of the covenant in blood and darkness – Genesis 15. The fact that the Living God would provide the only-begotten Son on Mount Moriah – Genesis 22. The whole system of priest and sacrifices of Exodus/Leviticus looking back to the promise of Genesis 22. The way that the Visible LORD mediates the Invisible LORD in the tent that is drenched in blood. The way of salvation is covered in blood and suffering throughout the Law and the Prophets. Every day innocent blood was shed in the tabernacle/temple to make atonement. In the Psalms the innocent, Righteous Messiah is constantly opposed, rejected, attacked by enemies and killed... yet always finally vindicated by His Father. The LORD constantly promises to achieve salvation even though He had to be pierced (Zechariah 12:10). He will come, filled with the Spirit, to bring justice for the oppressed, healing for the sick and injured, comfort for the grieving and He will spread this to all the nations. The LORD Himself is the Suffering Servant, the Great High Priest, the Lamb of God, the Crucified God who reigns from His Tree of cursed, atoning death, the resurrection of the Messiah and the subsequent resurrection of the dead and the New Creation.

and Jewish carpenters were at the bottom; money and influence were at the top and service and humility were at the bottom; status and power were at the top and mercy and gentleness were at the bottom. The Way of Jesus burst into that entrenched world and said that the Jewish carpenter not only made the universe but rules it from the highest heaven, that Caesar was a sinful man who would be judged by Jesus, that the greatest need was to be the slave of everybody else, that money should be used to help others and given away, that enemies should be loved rather than defeated, that slaves were equal to free in Jesus' kingdom. Yes, there is another king, high above all the presidents and prime ministers, far beyond the little empires and conglomerates, worth so much more than the banking systems and stock exchanges. Yes, there is another king who sees the world in almost the very opposite way that the kingdoms of this world see it. He invites the least and the weakest and the despised to His parties. He gives away His riches and walks the path of suffering service to eternal glory.

The crowd and the officials were stunned by the radical revolution of Jesus – verses 8-9. That little Thessalonian church was in for a tough time in such an environment. The kind of kingdom Jesus had and when it would be unveiled to the world became huge concerns to them and Paul had to write to them about these matters.[83] Paul and Silas had to leave them that very night and slipped away to Berea.

There was a synagogue in Berea so they began explaining the Scriptures straight away – verse 11.

It is clear that the Bereans were Luke's favourite people on the second missionary journey. "Now the Bereans were of more noble character than the Thessalonians, for they received the message with great eagerness and examined the Scriptures every day to see if what Paul said was true" (verse 12).

Many Christian organisations, especially in more Protestant circles, are named after the Bereans because of their great love for the clarity and authority of the Scriptures. No matter how brilliant or persuasive Paul might have seemed and no matter what signs and wonders he performed, yet they wanted to check everything he said by the Scriptures for themselves. It is a very good pattern to follow. When we listen to anyone explaining the Bible we should

---

83   For more on this see the Book by Book study material on Thessalonians.

always have a Bible open in front of us so we can examine the Scriptures to see if their teaching is true.

Many people claim to be teaching the Bible and may even make a great fuss about how much they love the Bible or how strong their ideas about the Bible are, but there are few people who simply teach the Bible and spend all the time and study necessary to explain it properly.

This atmosphere of Bible study appealed especially to the Jewish audience and many began to follow Jesus, along with some of the leading Berean women.

However, the Thessalonian trouble makers arrived and began to cause trouble. Before it turned nasty, the new Berean church helped Paul to slip away to Athens, whereas Silas and Timothy stayed on to help the Berean church get established – verses 13-15.

b. Athens (17:16-34)

Athens was a major city of the ancient world. It had been the centre of Greek civilisation for hundreds of years. Some of the greatest thinkers the world has ever known lived and taught in Athens. Systems of philosophy developed in Athens which even today continue to govern the basic patterns and structures of the academy. Greek theatre, which has had such a profound effect on European culture for two and a half thousand years, developed in Athens.

However, the apostle Paul's eyes had been radically changed by the upside-down kingdom of Jesus. Everything looks so different when judged from the cross of the Crucified God. Most tourists would have been filled with amazement at all the ancient temples honouring the gods who were so well known throughout the Greco-Roman world. Paul was just deeply upset and angry that a city of such greatness and influence was living under the stupid, wicked tyranny of man made gods – verse 16.[84]

---

84 The great Bible scholar Matthew Henry expresses this well: "A scholar that has acquaintance, and is in love, with the learning of the ancients, would think he should be very happy if he were where Paul now was, at Athens, in the midst of the various sects of philosophers, and would have a great many curious questions to ask them, for the explication of the remains we have of the Athenian learning; but Paul, though bred a scholar, and an ingenious active man, does not make this any of his business at Athens. He has other work to mind: it is not the improving of himself in their philosophy that he aims at, he has learned to call it a vain thing, and is above it (Col. 2:8); his business is, in God's name, to correct their disorders in religion, and to turn them from the service of idols, and of Satan in them, to the service of the true and living God in Christ."

To begin with Paul followed his normal practice of reasoning from the Scriptures in the synagogue – verse 17. Yet, he needed to reach the wider culture, the people who never went to the synagogue, the people who knew nothing of the ancient Hebrew Scriptures. He went to the market-place, possibly working as a leather-worker or tent maker, and reasoned with all the people there – verse 17.

A group of philosophers heard Paul's teaching about the resurrection and argued with him. Stoics were materialistic and viewed fate as the fundamental reality, governing humans and gods alike. The Epicureans were also materialists who focussed on the satisfaction of the physical senses and needs. The Stoics thought that there could be a kind of 'spiritual existence' beyond death but the Epicureans thought not.

It is easy to see why these two groups of philosophers reacted so strongly to news of the resurrection of Jesus. When we study the letters that Paul wrote to the nearby city of Corinth we get a glimpse into the problem they had with physical resurrection – 1 Corinthians 15. To the Greek mind, the human body had no possible future beyond death. The body dies and decays away. Nothing physical has any eternal significance. Spirits or 'minds' might ascend beyond this lowly level of existence to the pure realm of thought and mind, but there could be no future for the 'animal' body. Even the Corinthians who were trying to follow Jesus found it extremely hard to deal with, so we can be sure the same problems were at least as bad in Athens.[85]

The Stoics and Epicureans take Paul to their public debating area so that they could all hear more of Paul's ideas. However, far from respecting the great and ancient tradition of Greek philosophy, Luke dismisses that whole intellectual tradition in verse 21 – "All the Athenians and the foreigners who lived there spent their time doing nothing but talking about and listening to the latest ideas."

---

85 This narrow-minded Greek view of reality, elevating non-material life so much higher than physical life, had a terrible effect on the Christians with a background in Greek philosophy. A major problem arose in the 3rd-4th centuries when some thought that Jesus could not be as genuinely divine as the Father because He had become material. Pure deity could never become mixed up in material existence, therefore Jesus had to be a kind of divine creature. The Nicene Creed was formulated in 325 AD to deal with this strange view of reality.

Paul's speech at this Areopagus debating space is one of the most studied and debated aspects of the whole book of Acts. Some feel that ancient Athens, with its intellectual life and hedonistic, idolatrous culture bears so many connections to modern life that there are lessons to learn on how to share Jesus' new life today. Others feel that Paul is trying to establish a common ground – shared concern with 'religion' and poetry – and that he is able to make the Way of Jesus appealing by doing this. Others argue that whatever the success of Paul's speech, at least he was trying to connect with the Athenians with issues that they could engage with and see the relevance of.

However, when we consider Paul's reaction to Athenian culture in 17:16 it is not likely that he sees a concern for religion as something that unites Jesus and Athens. His opening words are not approving their religion, but condemning them for being so superstitious. The Greek word *deisidaimonesteros* is best translated by the phrase in the old King James Bible – "too superstitious".

Paul had looked at all the idols and statues. He had listened to their theories about the universe and religion. Now he gives the verdict. They don't even know what they are worshipping, so they end up worshipping anything and everything. They worshipped creatures and man-made ideas and idols without one scrap of genuine worship of the Living God. They even had an altar for any gods that they had missed! (verses 22-23).

So, Paul had news for them. Yes, they HAD missed a God – the Living God who made the heavens and the earth. The Greco-Roman gods were just part of the heavens and the earth. The universe already existed before they began.[86] Yet, says Paul, the Athenians needed to know about the Most High God who is so far above all these little objects of superstition and myths, the Supreme God who made even the highest heavens.

Those Greco-Roman gods needed human service and wanted humans to build temples for them. They needed the humans to serve them. Yet, what kind of gods are they? The True God does need anything from the human beings that He created. In fact, this Living God is the One who actually gives us all everything that we have and are. He causes the crops to grow, the seasons to remain, the sun to shine.

---

86   The Epicureans seemed to believe that the universe formed itself by random chance.

Paul is here paraphrasing 1 Kings 8:27, when Solomon says "will God really dwell on earth? The heavens, even the highest heaven, cannot contain you. How much less this temple I have built!" Everything that Paul says at the Areopagus is from the Hebrew Scriptures. Yet, because these philosophers were probably ignorant of the Scriptures he simply tells them what it says without telling them which prophet or king said it.

For example, the next thing Paul tells them is a summary of Genesis 5 and 10 where Adam is shown to have produced all the nations of the world. The Greeks may have believed that fate controlled everything, even the gods, but Paul explains that this Living God who made the heavens and the earth has not just abandoned it. Rather, in creating humanity from one man[87], He has actually determined where and when we all should live – verse 26.

Why? Why does this supremely powerful Creator bother to have such a detailed interest in humanity? Because He wants us to find Him. He has placed us all in situations where we can receive His life and blessings, where we receive His sun and rain, gaze up at His stars, feel His life coursing through us, look at one another and see His image gazing back at us.

The Living God wants to be found by us, so He hides in plain sight, right in front of us, in all the details and moments of life.[88] We are constantly surrounded by this Living God in all we do, all we think, all we say.

Paul even quotes from an Athenian poet who suggested that we are the offspring of God.[89] In quoting this pagan poet Paul is challenging the Athenians: "if you really thought like that then how could you ever imagine that the gods were like gold or silver or stone. A little inanimate statue made

---

87 It may well have been important for the Greeks to learn that all humanity is just one family, that we are all distant relatives. Most ancient (and modern) empires and cultures tended to assume other humans were lesser creatures than themselves.

88 The great African theologian, Athanasius, says that the Invisible God is made so visible in the world around us that it is obvious to everybody that He is mediated by His Divine Word. "So it was open to them, by looking into the height of heaven, and perceiving the harmony of creation, to know its Ruler, the Word of the Father, Who, by His own providence over all things makes known the Father to all, and to this end moves all things, that through Him all may know God." *Incarnation of the Word*, chapter 12. Only God can reveal God, so it must be the Divine Word/Son who upholds and sustains the creation that reveals the Unseen God through the creature.

89 This was probably Aratus, from Paul's home region near Tarsus, who says that we are the offspring of Jupiter (who was worshipped as the supreme god).

by a craftsman is obviously far inferior to a living, breathing, thinking, acting human being. Surely whoever produced all this is vastly more than us rather than less than us? (verses 28-29).

The Living God could have destroyed us all long ago for these offences against Him, refusing to give them the honour and gratitude He deserves for all He has done for us and all He has given us. Rather He patiently waited – verse 30. However, now He is sending out messengers around the whole world to tell everybody to turn around, leave behind all the superstitious idols and ideas, and turn towards the True God. He has set a deadline for this, a day when He will judge the whole world. This day of Divine Justice will all be handled by the man who has gone through death and come out the other side into physical, human immortality. This man claimed that He was the final Judge for the whole world and He said that He wanted to claim all the nations of the world. These claims were proved to be right when He conquered death itself – verses 29-31.

However, the Athenians had already made their mind up that resurrection wasn't possible. They were prisoners of their superstitions and they either sneered at the message or thought it might be nice to hear some more. Nevertheless a few were ready to follow Jesus right away – verse 34 – including Dionysius and Damaris.

> Though some people see this speech of Paul as a failure, yet on examination, Paul's speech was brilliant in that he started with creation, ended with New Creation. He showed that the Living God is Creator and Sustainer of all things; that he directs the paths of all people and wants to be found by all people; that he calls people to repent and will send his chosen servant to judge people one day in the future. He has encapsulated the key elements of the Biblical gospel in a way that pagan people can understand.

Although some had asked to hear more from Paul, as far as He was concerned they had already had their chance. Paul left Athens and went to Corinth. This is sobering. People always assume that they can get around to it tomorrow or look into the matter when they have time. We never know when the opportunity to follow Jesus will be the last opportunity.

c. Corinth (18:1-17)

Corinth was such a prosperous, cosmopolitan city largely due to geography. By sailing from the Adriatic Sea into the Corinthian Gulf, goods could be sent across the narrow strip of land of Corinth and transported on from Cenchrea to the Aegean Sea.

When Paul arrived in Corinth there were Jewish refugees from Rome, ordered out by Emperor Claudius – verse 2. Paul met a husband and wife team of fellow tent-makers/leather workers called Aquila and Priscilla. They were originally from an area of north-eastern Asia Minor called Pontus, on the Black Sea coast. This internationally well-travelled couple were happy for Paul to join them in the business and share their accommodation – verse 3. This couple were to become life-long friends of Paul, later travelling with him to Ephesus, instructing Apollos (see verse 26) and eventually returning to Rome (see Romans 16:3). At the end of his life Paul made sure to send greetings to them – 2 Timothy 4:19.

With a regular source of income, Paul was able to settle in Corinth, teaching both Jews and internationals in the synagogue – verse 4. When Silas and Timothy arrived, he focussed exclusively on teaching the Corinthian Jews that Jesus is the Messiah. However, when opposition and abuse began, he brushed off the dust in protest and went next door to the house of a Gentile called Titius Justus.

It was a confrontational situation! The ruler of the synagogue was a follower of Jesus and the Jesus movement was rapidly expanding with internationals in the house right next door to the synagogue! Paul must have felt a little nervous because Jesus came to Paul in a vision and told him not to be afraid. The reference to having many people in this city is best taken to be an encouragement that there were already a number of believers in the city. Jesus commissioned him to keep on sharing His new life in Corinth, promising that Paul would not be harmed – verse 10. Paul stayed on for 18 months[90], writing two letters to the Thessalonian church – 1 & 2 Thessalonians.

---

90   As a point of interest, Church history records that the apostle Thomas was killed by Brahmin priests at this time. While the new life of Jesus was moving westward along the Mediterranean, this world revolution had been travelling in other directions too.

Luke gives one example of how the LORD Jesus protected Paul from harm. The unbelieving Jews dragged Paul before the proconsul – verses 12-13 – with the accusation that Paul was undermining the Law of Moses. Gallio was a Roman pagan and a skilled politician. What did he care about some internal dispute among the followers of one religion or another? That was their own business – verse 15.[91] The Jews were thrown out and they were so embarrassed and annoyed that they turned on the new synagogue ruler called Sosthenes (who presumably had incited this 'legal action') – verse 17.[92]

Eventually Paul had to return to Antioch in Syria. It had been a long missionary journey and he needed to report back to his home church. Paul must have been on some kind of Nazirite vow because before sailing from Cenchrea[93] he shaved off his hair[94] – verse 18. This special vow could be taken on for a limited time when a person wanted to be especially dedicated to the LORD. Perhaps his Nazirite vow of special commitment had covered the time of his mission in Corinth, asking for special blessing and protection.

The final city on this second missionary journey was Ephesus. Again Paul taught in the synagogue and received a warm reception. Aquila and Priscilla remained there while Paul, promising to return soon if God willed it – verse 21, sailed for Caesarea before arriving back at Antioch.

d. The Third Missionary Journey (18:23-21:9)

After such a long and involved mission, Paul took time to reconnect to his home church, yet while he did this Aquila and Priscilla were making things happen in Ephesus.

---

91   He dismisses the whole matter as "questions about words and names", presumably referring to the question of whether Jesus was the Messiah.

92   By the time that Paul wrote his first letter to the Corinthians, it seems that Sosthenes had become a Christian – 1 Cor. 1:1

93   In Romans 16:1 we learn that there was a church in Cenchrea served by a woman called Phoebe.

94   See Numbers 6. Obviously, Jesus grew up in the town of the Nazirites, indicating the dedicating commitment shown by Mary and Joseph. It is entirely possible that Jesus had spent most of His life on a Nazirite vow, which is why they mocked Him by offering Him wine/vinegar on the Cross.

A North African Jew from Alexandria, called Apollos, arrived at Ephesus.[95] He knew the Scriptures well, but it seems that he had heard only the message of John the Baptist that Jesus was going was the Messiah. It is likely that he had not yet heard what had happened to Jesus with respect to His death, resurrection, ascension and the gift of the Spirit to foreigners as well as Jews. The same problem that Apollos had was widespread in Ephesus – 19:1-7.

When Aquila and Priscilla heard Apollos they realised he needed to be brought up to speed on all that had happened to Jesus and the global expansion of Israel, so they gave him a place to stay while they instructed him – 18:26. Before Apollos could really teach his updated message in Ephesus he wanted to head across to Corinth (in Achaia) where he held public debates, proving from the Scriptures that Jesus is the Messiah. He became very influential in Corinth.[96]

Luke tells us all this so that we see how the international family of Jesus was spreading and growing and learning even when the apostle Paul had left them. Once the new life of Jesus was delivered to a city, the local church would set down roots and begin their own mission work.

Back in Antioch Paul was ready for another international mission. He travelled through Asia Minor, visiting all the different international churches.

The book of Acts began with 120 Jewish disciples taking the first shaky steps out of their meeting room and already the entire focus has changed to a mission going on in many different regions, with people from many different nations and continents, whether Asia, Africa or Europe.

---

95 Alexandria had a large Jewish population and had a well developed expectation of the coming Messiah. It is easy to see why John the Baptist was so well received in Alexandria with its deep roots in Bible study and Messianic hope. Philo was the leading Bible teacher in Alexandria and his understanding of the second person of the Trinity was so wonderfully rich before he knew anything of the events of the New Testament. For example, *Who is Heir?* (205) "…the Father has given the Word, his eldest and chief messenger the special privilege of standing at the border separating the creature from the Creator. On the one hand, he is ever with the Incorruptible (God) as intercessor for the perishing mortal and, on the other, (he is) the ambassador of the Head to the subject."

96 See for example 1 Cor. 1:12; 3:4-6, 22. Paul taught him the importance of sticking to the text of Scripture alone – 1 Cor. 4:6. Later, Apollos was told to go back to Corinth by Paul, even though he didn't want to – 1 Cor. 16:12. We also know that he passed through Crete – Titus 3:13.

e. Ephesus (19:1-41)

When Paul eventually arrived at the far western coast of Asia Minor he returned to Ephesus. He had only very briefly spoken to them before on his way back to Antioch, but now he got to know all the different people in that extraordinary city.

Apollos had gone to Corinth but Apollos' problem was more widespread in Ephesus. Paul found twelve men who had heard John the Baptist's message about the coming of the Messiah (verse 4), but had not heard the conclusion of the story that Jesus is that Promised Messiah. They still need to hear about His death, resurrection, ascension and the global spread of Israel. They were still at the God-fearing stage, living as Gentiles on the edge of the Jewish community. The fact that there was a Holy Spirit and that this Holy Spirit was available to everybody, of every nation was news to them – verses 2-5. Paul brought them up to speed, baptised them into the Name of Jesus and then they too were filled with the Spirit and began preaching in their native languages.

As in Corinth, the teaching work began in the synagogue but after three months due to opposition from some unbelieving Jews, Paul shifted venue to a public lecture hall – verses 8-9. This meant that instead of teaching once a week on the Sabbath, he was able to teach every day for two years! Such a sustained presentation of the Way of Jesus meant that "all the Jews and non-Jews who lived in the province of Asia heard the word of the Lord" – verse 10.

The Living God authenticated the apostle's message with incredible miracles, just like the ones that had accompanied the other apostles back in Acts 5:12-16. It was as if Jesus Himself was at ministering and teaching in this pagan, international city.

Seven Jewish brothers of the Sceva priestly family noticed the power in the Name of Jesus and used it to control demons – verse 13. They got away with it for a while, but when they came up against a serious evil spirit they were answered back – "Jesus I know and I know about Paul, but who are you?". They were stripped naked and beaten up, bringing them right down to size, taking away all their dignity and arrogance.

What is so striking about this is the fact that the evil spirit knew about Paul. We can understand how he knew of Jesus, the LORD of heaven and earth, but

Paul was also known to the spirits. How close to Jesus are we? Is our teaching so faithful, our service so sacrificial, our giving so generous, our prayers so faithful, our love so practical that the spirits know us too?

The city of Ephesus was very concerned with spirits, gods and superstition so this incident had a profound affect – verse 17. Some of the 'believers' had retained their occult practices. They confessed their sin and publicly burned all their occult books and scrolls.[97] They could see the head-on collision between Jesus and these spiritual forces.[98] All this made people realise that the Way of Jesus was not just a theory but a life revolution changing the world – verse 20. While staying at Ephesus Paul wrote his first letter to the Corinthian church – see 1 Corinthians 16:5-9.

Paul made plans to return to Jerusalem after going on to Greece and then take the new life of Jesus even further – to Rome. He was ready to cross yet another sea and go even further, to the very heart of the Empire. While Timothy and Erastus went ahead, Paul stayed a little longer around Ephesus – verse 22. However, in that short time a big crisis happened – 19:23-41.

As long as the Christians continued to secretly carry on buying and treasuring the occult products, nobody worried about the Way of Jesus. When it became clear that following Jesus was actually going to change the way people lived, how they spent their money, what they invested in, then it became serious.

Christians can always have a quiet life if they just talk about things far away in heaven and in the distant future/past. However, when they follow Jesus' teaching and start rocking the boat about money, justice, sex, investments and service, then the powers of this age know that there is a serious threat.

Demetrius the silversmith organised the major industry of silver models of Artemis (the goddess Diana). He called a special meeting warning that the Way of Jesus would quickly destroy this profitable business. His accusation against Paul is so delightfully absurd – "He says that man-made gods are no

---

97   These occult items were valued at 50,000 drachmas. A drachma was a day's wage, so we could calculate the value at 160 years wages. At the time of writing this would amount to more than £3.5 million.

98   When Paul writes to the Ephesian church he has so much to tell them about their position high above these spiritual forces – Ephesians 1:19b-23. He also instructs them on the nature of this 'spiritual battle' – Ephesians 6:10-18.

gods at all" – verse 26.[99] Demetrius felt that they had a good reputation for making these man-made gods and was concerned that "the great goddess Artemis... will be robbed of her divine majesty" (verses 26-27). It is clear that a Divine Being was being robbed of their divine majesty, but it wasn't Artemis.[100]

Nevertheless, the crowd was so alarmed that they began mindlessly shouting "Great is Artemis of the Ephesians". They grabbed a couple of Paul's travelling companions and the whole mob moved into the public theatre. The Ephesian church leaders and even regional officials from the area prevented passionate, confrontational Paul from wading into the assembly – verses 30-31. It seems that a spiritual darkness had confused the massive crowd because "most of the people didn't even know why they were there" – verse 32.

The unbelieving Jews felt there was an opportunity to control the crowd in their interests and pushed a character called Alexander to the front.[101] However, the Jewish legalists were also set against Artemis so they finally all united in shouting their great slogan, "Great is Artemis of the Ephesians" for two hours! The only response of paganism to Jesus is irrational shouting and mindless chanting.

The city clerk was a man of great wisdom – verses 35-41. He made four powerful points to the mob before dismissing them:

1. The world knew that Ephesus was the guardian of the temple of Artemis and had sole rights of selling her image – verses 35-36.

2. These men had not robbed or blasphemed. They were not interested in producing cheap fake images of Artemis – verse 37.

3. Demetrius can take legal action if there is a genuine offence – verses 38-39.

4. The crowd was in danger of causing criminal offence – verse 40.

---

99 Paul had certainly made this point to the Athenians, However when speaking about idolatry within the 'Lord's people' Isaiah was very severe on this subject – Isaiah 40:18-26; 41:7, 21-24.

100 The temple to Artemis was one of the largest temples in the whole ancient world and people came from all over the world to see it. In later centuries it became the site of a Christian church.

101 It is possible that this is Alexander the metal-worker (silver-smith?) who Paul refers to in 2 Timothy 4:14.

Perhaps a good lesson from this is to avoid blaspheming different religions. Our main job is to positively present the Way of Jesus, which reveals the problems of all other systems of belief. When speaking to fellow 'believers' the ancient prophets denounced their pagan practices with very harsh ridicule, but they did not spend much time doing this towards the pagan nations. Rather than draw attention to the other religious systems and force people to become defensive about those ideas and practices, it seems much wiser to show the infinitely better way of new life in Jesus.

f.   Travelling to Jerusalem (20:1-38)

Luke provides a very brief summary of the months that Paul spent in Macedonia and Greece,[102] but he wanted us to see something of the variety of companions that Paul collected on this missionary journey:

- Luke himself joined the group – note 'us' in verse 5.
- Sopater, son of Pyrrhus was from the Berean church.
- Aristarchus[103] & Secundus from the Thessalonian church.
- Gaius from the church at Derbe.
- Timothy from Lystra.
- Tychicus and Trophimus from the region around Ephesus.

This list is a thrilling demonstration of the international character of the global family of Jesus. Israel had gone from being a defensive island in a sea of pagan nations to being a tidal wave of the life of God sweeping over all these nations. Paul must have been so encouraged to look around at this group of people from around the eastern Mediterranean, representing different nations and cultures, speaking different native languages, yet all redeemed into God's global family. The hesitations of the circumcision party seem so far away!

The whole team regrouped at Troas where they gathered with the local church to break bread together on Sunday – verse 7. Paul must have had a

---

102   While travelling in the region Paul was taking up a collection to provide help for the churches in Judea – see 1 Corinthians 16:1-5; Romans 15:25-33; 2 Cor. 8-9.

103   In Acts 27:2 we see Aristarchus travelling with Paul again.

great deal to teach because he was still speaking at midnight when a young man called Eutychus fell asleep and was killed as he slipped from his third storey window ledge (verses 7-9). Paul quickly went downstairs and (as Peter had done with Tabitha – Acts 9:36-43) raised him back to life.

Perhaps Paul wanted time alone so he walked to Assos whereas the companions went by ship – verses 12-14). Paul was keen to get to Jerusalem for Pentecost so the Ephesian church leaders met the apostolic team at Miletus, where Paul gave them his moving farewell speech.

He began by reminding them of his life and service in that province of Asia. Under severe opposition Paul lived as Jesus lived, humbly serving them. He made sure that everybody, regardless of national or religious background, had been challenged to turn around and follow Jesus – verses 18-21. He knew that there was some kind of serious suffering waiting for him in Jerusalem. In every city the Holy Spirit gave people prophecies telling him about this. Yet, he had no interest in avoiding this future – verse 24. Just as Jesus had set His face towards Jerusalem to face His suffering, Paul was doing exactly the same. Though he wouldn't see them again, he knew he could leave them with a clear conscience having done all he could to help them in the Way of Jesus – verses 25-27.

Now that he was leaving, the full pastoral responsibility of the churches in the region fell on them.

> Keep watch over yourselves and all the flock of which the Holy Spirit has made you overseers. *Be shepherds of the church of God, which he bought with his own blood* – Acts 20:28.

1. They had to watch over their own walk with Jesus as a top priority. They would be no help to others if they had strayed away from the Way of Jesus and had turned into one of the wolves who harmed the flock.

2. They had to watch over the flock, which is the heart of church leadership. Whatever else the local church may do, whatever wider plans of action and visions it pursues, the foundational responsibility is to the brothers and sisters in the church family. We need to be protected from false teaching, encouraged into daily practical service and equipped for all the work that the family of Jesus needs to do together.

3. Ultimately it is the Holy Spirit who raises up leaders in the church family. He gives the gifts and the love needed for the work.

4. The church is so very precious. It is God's answer to the problems of the world. He shed His own blood to buy the church. What a price tag! How inconceivably precious is the blood of the Eternal God! The blood of the infinite and immortal LORD God who inhabits eternity was poured out to pay for these redeemed international communities all around the world.

Yet, savage wolves are out to destroy the precious church – verses 29-31. The very worst of the wolves will come from within the church family, those who pretend to follow Jesus, speak the right words, give the right answers, but do not have the unmistakeable fruit that Jesus tells us to watch for. Paul spent three years constantly warning about these dangers – verse 31.

As Paul has imitated Jesus, so he now tells the Ephesian leaders to imitate him – verses 32-35. As Paul had no interest in money or possessions, so we should forget all interest in acquiring money. Paul always tried to avoid taking any money from anybody – verse 34. In following Jesus in a lifestyle of giving rather than taking, they would help all those who are weak or needy.[104]

Knowing what Paul had said about never seeing them again, his departure was full of long embraces and wet faces – verses 36-38.

---

[104] John told us that Jesus said and did many things that are not recorded (John 21:25), and these words of Jesus in Acts 20:35 are not recorded in any of the four official biographies. It is a little treasure of extra teaching from Jesus that the Spirit wanted to preserve.

Study 8   Bible Questions

Acts 20:13-38

1. Verses 13-17 – Why didn't Paul want to go to Ephesus himself on this journey? Why was he in a hurry to get to Jerusalem?

2. Verses 18-21 – How does Paul describe the way he conducted himself whilst he was in Asia? What was the heart of his message and to whom?

3. Verses 22-24 – What lies ahead for Paul and what is his major concern?

4. Verses 25-27 – Why does Paul tell the elders of the Ephesian church that he is innocent of the blood of all men? What does this mean?

5. Verses 28-31 – Summarise the sort of attitude that Paul tells the elders they should adopt. What did they have to watch for?

6. Verses 32-35 – In what ways has Paul's life in Asia mirrored that of Jesus? Which group of people had Paul been concerned about?

7. Verses 36-38 – What would life be like for the churches in Asia without having Paul around? What does the reaction of the elders tell us about the way they thought of Paul?

8. Verses 13-38 – How does this passage help us to identify the right sort of people who should be in church leadership? How does it help us as members of congregations to know what to expect of those who are over us in the Lord? What leadership positions should this passage apply to?

Study 8	Further Questions

Why were the believers at Berea commended? How can we adopt the same attitude as they had? How can we make this more possible in our churches and when we meet together with other Christians?

Was Paul's speech in Athens a success or a failure? Why?

The believers at Ephesus made a very significant statement about their transformed life as believers in Jesus burning a huge amount of their magic books and showing that they were leaving that old life behind them. What actions did you make or do you continue to make to demonstrate your commitment to the new life? What could you dispose of or stop watching or stop doing today that would be evidence that you have left your old life behind you?

Are the sorts of miracles that God did through Paul in Ephesus (19:11-12) to be expected today? Why? What was their purpose then?

Study 8	Daily Readings
Day 1	Acts 17
Day 2	Acts 18
Day 3	Acts 19
Day 4	Acts 20
Day 5	1 Thessalonians 1
Day 6	1 Corinthians 1
Day 7	Ephesians 1

The daily Bible readings are an opportunity to not only read through all of the material in the book under study, but also to read parts of the Bible that relate to the themes and issues that we have been considering. We try to make sure that we receive light from the whole Bible as we think through the key issues each week.

Paul the Revolutionary

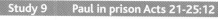

Study 9   Paul in prison Acts 21-25:12

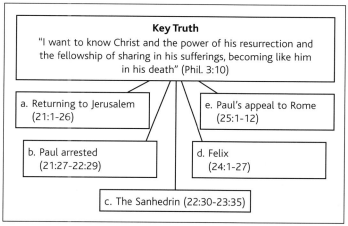

Key Truth
"I want to know Christ and the power of his resurrection and the fellowship of sharing in his sufferings, becoming like him in his death" (Phil. 3:10)

a. Returning to Jerusalem (21:1-26)

e. Paul's appeal to Rome (25:1-12)

b. Paul arrested (21:27-22:29)

d. Felix (24:1-27)

c. The Sanhedrin (22:30-23:35)

a. Returning to Jerusalem (21:1-26)

With prophecies promising suffering for Paul in Jerusalem, like his Lord, he set his face towards Jerusalem. The journey from Miletus took them to Cos, Rhodes, Patar, by Cyprus and onto Tyre – 21:1-3. Even after they landed, the local Christians had also received prophecies from the Spirit about Paul's coming sufferings and they pleaded with him not to go to Jerusalem. The similarities with the life of Jesus are striking.

After an emotional prayer time on the beach – verse 5 – they continued on to Caesarea via Ptolemais where they stayed with Philip and his four preaching daughters – verse 9.[105] Agabus, who had accurately predicted the famine in Acts 11:28, arrived to give an enacted prophecy of the trouble that awaited Paul in Jerusalem – verses 10-11.

Agabus' enacted prophecy had such an impact on the followers of Jesus that Luke joined in with the others in pleading with Paul not to go to Jerusalem – verse 12.

---

105   1 Cor. 11:4-5.

There is such a profound collision between the kingdoms and values of this age and the kingdom of Jesus. If we judge our lives and success according to the flesh then suffering and pain must be avoided and pleasure and comfort must be pursued. Some say this principle is almost wired into our basic instincts in this passing age. The Way of Jesus teaches us the very opposite. Jesus teaches us that we find our life only when we lose our life for His sake.

> Jesus said to his disciples, "If anyone would come after me, he must deny himself and take up his cross and follow me. For whoever wants to save his life will lose it, but whoever loses his life for me will find it" (Matthew 16:24-25)

Only when we accept that each day we are living as if we were about to die; only when we give our lives away in Jesus' name as if we were about to lose them anyway; only when we ignore the security, status and treasure that this world offers and invest in people for Jesus' glory; only when we count suffering for Jesus as the very greatest honour that we could ever receive; only when we put the interests of others always ahead of our own interests... only in such a new life, such a divine life from Jesus, will we find that joy and life and peace and fruitfulness that is the secret of the Living God.

When we have to accept that we have nothing and when we are at the end of our tether and unconditionally surrender to Jesus, to His Way and Life, then we finally begin to live.

Jesus had taught Paul this truth not only in Arabia but through these missionary journeys. When Paul lived in luxurious, decadent, wealthy Corinth yet worked night and day so that he didn't need to take any money from them, he was learning that the real treasures are not what the flesh thinks. When Paul saw how the Ephesian silver trade sent people into a kind of madness through greed and superstition, he could appreciate the sanity that Jesus gives to those who abandon all for Him. When he saw how religious leaders fell so easily in bitter, destructive jealousy, he realised how vital it was to be the humble slave who has crucified self.

Following Jesus and obeying His commands will always turn the world upside down. It will always cause people to dismiss us as extremists, as followers of a 'social gospel', as fundamentalists, as hippies, as bigots, as idealists, as too doctrinaire, as too concerned with 'works' or any number of other accusations delivered with either apparent care or open hatred. If we are determined to trust Jesus and walk His narrow path of practical faith and love with understanding, then we can only know a life of being attacked by fellow 'Christians', by enemies of the faith, by wolves within the church and devils outside.

If we are going to follow Jesus whatever the cost and refuse to conform to the patterns of this world, then we too will have to face the choice that Paul faces in Acts 21 – walking into a future with courage, love and trust knowing that suffering awaits us.

Yes, his brothers and sisters in Jesus loved Paul and couldn't bear the thought of him suffering when he had served them with such love. Of course they were protective of him. Yet, Paul could see that he was being granted a very great honour of walking to suffering in Jerusalem just as Jesus had done.

> Paul answered, "Why are you weeping and breaking my heart? I am ready not only to be bound, but also to die in Jerusalem for the name of the Lord Jesus" (Acts 21:13)

His companions saw that the only safe response to this is the response that Jesus gave in the Garden of Gethsemane – "The Lord's will be done" (verse 14). On the way to Jerusalem they stayed with one of the earliest disciples, perhaps one of the 120 who had been present in Acts chapter 1 – a Cypriot called Mnason.

As readers of the missionary journeys of Paul, we have been around the Mediterranean world with him meeting people of so many nationalities and languages. We have seen people wonderfully welcomed by the Holy Spirit into Jesus' global family. We have seen the world turned upside down as the Kingdom of Jesus has burst into all the different Gentile cities.

This is why we are so shocked by the news given to Paul after his reports were received with such joy (verses 17-19) – "many thousands of Jews have believed, and all of them are zealous for the law. They have been informed that you teach all the Jews who live among the Gentiles to turn away from Moses, telling them not to circumcise their children or live according to our customs. What shall we do?"

After spending so many chapters in the global revolution of Jesus around Asia Minor, Macedonia and Greece, it seems such a weird echo of a bygone age to hear that there were thousands who were still trying to digest what Jesus was actually doing all around the world. By this time there were growing churches in the Indian sub-continent, Africa, Asia and Europe. Back at Jerusalem, where it all started, the process seemed to be stuck or even going into reverse. However, if we remember that for 1,500 years the church had been thinking in terms of a geographical boundary, confined by the terms of the Sinai covenant, then we can perhaps understand why some of the Jewish followers of Jesus were taking longer to grasp that the temporary time of Moses' law was over.

James and the Jerusalem elders were worried for Paul so they thought it might be good for Paul to make a public show of his respect for the law of Moses. We can sense something of the nervousness of the Jerusalem leaders here, eager to appease the powerful and fanatical Judeans who had not yet grasped the significance of Jesus. We might even say that the Jerusalem leaders were still not fully clear on what was happening elsewhere and were more concerned for customs, than for the radical transformation that was taking over the world away from Jerusalem.

Presumably in connection with the Nazirite vow of Numbers 6, Paul joined a group of men going to the temple for purification. In Acts 18:18 Paul ended a vow, so he may well have ended another Nazirite vow at this time too.

b. Paul arrested (21:27-22:29)

Before the Nazirite vow purification time was over, Jews from the province of Asia (probably from Ephesus) saw Paul. Paul had been seen in Jerusalem with a man called Trophimus, from Ephesus (21:29). Perhaps these Judean agitators remembered Trophimus from Ephesus, but they knew he was a Gentile (21:28). When Paul was in the temple, preparing for the end of the purification period, the Ephesian Jews got the idea that Paul had brought Trophimus into the temple as an act of sacrilege! In these fever pitch atmospheres all kinds of strange ideas take on a life of their own.

In fact it was the Asian Jews who caused trouble at the temple and their accusations against Paul are worth studying. There are two main accusations. First that Paul had been teaching everybody everywhere against our people and our Law and "this place". The narrow tribalism in this accusation is easy to detect. The second accusation is deeper. They were concerned that Paul was bringing Gentiles to the temple. In Matthew 21:13 Jesus had complained about the way that the Jewish authorities excluded people from the temple area and Jesus quoted from Isaiah 56:6-7.

> "*foreigners* who bind themselves to the LORD to serve him, to love the name of the LORD, and to worship him, all who keep the Sabbath without desecrating it and who hold fast to my covenant – these I will bring to my holy mountain and give them joy in my house of prayer. Their burnt offerings and sacrifices will be accepted on my altar; for my house will be called a house of prayer for *all nations*."

Jesus the Messiah, the One to whom the temple truly belonged, wanted the temple to be a place for people of all nations to come to the Living God. The Judeans, with their focus on OUR people and OUR Law, were going in the opposite direction to the LORD God of Israel. It is not too much to say that this temple had reached the end of its useful life.

The people who were supposed to represent the Living God were turned into a bloodthirsty mob and only the intervention of a Gentile army commander prevented a terrible crime being committed – (verses 30-32). Once the crowd saw this Gentile enter the temple area they took a far more humble and passive approach! (verse 32).

Just as the accusations against Jesus had been confused and contradictory, so they were against Paul also (verse 34). Just as Jesus had been bound, just as the mob shouted for Jesus' murder, so Paul was given the great honour of the same treatment in the same place (verse 36).

Jesus told us to be as wise as serpents yet as harmless as doves (Matthew 10:16) and Paul showed this so well. To the Roman commander he spoke in Greek (verse 37) but to the crowd he spoke in Aramaic (verse 40). By connecting with the Roman commander Paul was able to put matters straight about who he really was (verse 39). The Roman commander had assumed Paul was an Egyptian terrorist who had led an armed revolution.

Perhaps the crowd also thought Paul was the Egyptian terrorist but when they heard him speaking to them in Aramaic, appealing to them as "brothers and fathers', they became quiet (22:2).

It was already very clear that his identity was extremely important in this situation. Rather than engage in a theological lecture or even an impassioned rhetorical argument, Paul simply tells his own story. He began by establishing his Jewish credentials. Yes, he was born in Tarsus, but he was not only raised in Jerusalem but also trained under the eminent Gamaliel in the law. There could be no doubt as to his thorough training in the Law of Moses.

However, what if he was studying for mere academic interest? No, said Paul. He was "just as zealous for God as" any of the people in the mob. Paul's comment here is double-edged. They would agree that they were very zealous for God, yet Paul's evidence for 'zeal' here is persecution and murder. Yes, Paul had once had the same kind of deluded 'zeal' for God that produced the most evil and ungodly actions.

Paul actually cited the high priest and the Council as his character references (verse 5). He had worked for them as an enforcer, dragging people to Jerusalem for punishment. How could anyone deny that Paul had proved that he had more "legal zeal" than anyone else? If Paul was acting in a way that they could not understand, they had to see that he was not acting out of ignorance or hatred of the law.

So what had happened to change a man like this? Paul explained that the Lord Jesus of Nazareth had appeared to him in divine glory (verses 5-11). Paul explained that he had been sent by Jesus to see a man who was a "devout observer of the law and highly respected by all the Jews living" in Damascus" (verse 12). Far from directing Paul away from the LORD God of "our ancestors" (verse 14), Ananias explained that Paul was to work for the "God of our ancestors" and to see the Righteous One.

This is almost certainly a reference to the powerful prophecy from Isaiah about the fact that the whole world will be brought to worship the LORD (Isaiah 24:14-16):

"from the west they acclaim the LORD's majesty. Therefore in the east give glory to the LORD; exalt the name of the LORD, the God of Israel, in the islands of the sea. From the ends of the earth we hear singing: "Glory to the Righteous One.""

As the servant of this Righteous One Paul had to go to the nations to tell them all about Him (Acts 22:15). To mark the beginning of this new work Paul was ceremonially washed (verse 16) and travelled to Jerusalem to pray at the temple.

Paul was showing how all his instincts and affections were fixed on the Law and the temple. Yet, in the temple the LORD told him to leave Jerusalem because the people of Jerusalem would not accept this message. Rather, Paul was sent to tell the nations of the Righteous One, just as Isaiah had prophesied.

The reaction of the crowd (verses 22-23) was so intense that it reminds us how important this issue is. As we look around the world we see 'religion' defined by geography and culture. The world religions are products of specific human cultures, languages, styles and regions. Outsiders are compelled to forsake their own culture if they are going to join the world religions. The Way of Jesus is so very different, standing in opposition to all human religion. If even the Law revealed through Moses at Sinai could be turned into a merely human religion of geography and exclusion then we all need to be so very careful. The sinful human heart will always want to turn to the comfortable ways of religion that lie under human control. Jesus the LORD God rejects all that and sends His followers out into the whole world, ready to serve others, ready to leave their own cultural treasures for the sake of serving others. When we die to ourselves and trust Jesus alone then we are lifted into the wide open space of Jesus where people of every language and culture can find genuine unity in all their diversity, where religion is left behind and life really begins, where truth is founded on love, where knowledge is tempered by patience.

Due to the intensity of the crowd's reaction the Roman commander concluded that Paul needed serious investigation and ordered that Paul be flogged to make him more open to questioning (verse 24). Totalitarian regimes always use cruelty, torture and violence to enforce their rule.

However, when Paul questioned the legality of beating a Roman citizen the commander was astonished. What he had paid so much to get, Paul had by birth, for free. So many of us have legal privileges that may provide so much protection and advantage for the Way of Jesus. Perhaps we live in societies where we are still free to live and speak the Way of Jesus. Perhaps we have the freedom to write to the governments and jails where our brothers and sisters are kept in prison. Perhaps we have the freedom and resources to support and sponsor gospel workers around the world. Perhaps we have the legal skills and opportunity to fight for justice for the widows, orphans and poor around the world… or around the corner.

c. The Sanhedrin (22:30-23:35)

The commander (Claudius Lysias) obviously felt out of his depth so released Paul and summoned the Sanhedrin, the chief priests and the high priest himself. Why were they so determined to kill this Roman citizen?

Paul spoke directly to these religious leaders and explained that he had been faithfully serving the Living God – 23:1. Such a claim was so inflammatory because it seemed blasphemous to them that a follower of Jesus would dare to claim to be faithful to 'their' God.

Ananias, the high priest ordered that Paul be struck in the face and Paul responded with a severe rebuke – verse 3. Was Paul's eyesight so bad that he couldn't recognise Ananias – verse 5? It is more likely that Paul could not believe that the high priest would dare to speak against Jesus.

Paul explained that he didn't realise that Ananias was the high priest because, as Exodus 22:28 states, it is forbidden to speak evil against the LORD's Messiah and surely the high priest would never speak against the LORD's Anointed King. In 2 Samuel 19:21 we see the law of Exodus 22:28 applied against Shimei because he spoke against David even though David was nothing more than an earthly representative of the true Anointed King. Paul is so shocked that Ananias speaks against the true Anointed King, the Divine Ruler of the people, that Paul can't imagine that this man could really be the high priest.

Jesus Himself had stood before the Sanhedrin and they had condemned Him to death. Paul could hardly expect a better reception. This was a very frightening and intimidating experience for the apostle.

Throughout these chapters Paul has to give an account of himself on five occasions. It is important to see how this humble and holy servant of Jesus faced all these challenges. One small man faced with such opposition may have resorted to despair or politics. However, what we find is a man who has learned to trust in Jesus as the LORD God of heaven and earth.

The Pharisees and the Sadducees were theological opponents. The Sadducees were materialists, rejecting the existence of angels or any resurrection life – see verse 8. The blessings they were looking for were the blessings of money and influence in this life. The Pharisees, for all their faults, were more faithful to the Scriptures in that they accepted the resurrection, judgement day and angels just as the Hebrew Scriptures presented these matters.

As Paul faced the Sanhedrin we can see that these two groups within Judaism were attempting to portray the followers of Jesus as a group that was outside the faith of Israel. It was vitally important that this did not happen. Jesus is the Jewish Messiah that the Hebrew Scriptures constantly speak about. He is the One that Moses was writing about – John 1:45.

In order to break up the ungodly coalition of the Pharisees and the Sadducees, Paul explains that he was from the Pharisee group and that his preaching of the resurrection of the dead had got him into this trouble – verse 6. Technically this was true. However, it was Paul's preaching of the resurrection of Jesus in particular that had attracted so much opposition rather than general ideas about future resurrection.

The Pharisees wanted to defend Paul. Perhaps his encounter on the road to Damascus had been an angel or spirit? – verse 9. Jesus acknowledged that the Pharisees studied the Scriptures diligently even though they did not come to Jesus – John 5:39-40. However, Jesus is even more dismissive of the Sadducees when He says that they knew neither the Scriptures nor the power of God – Mark 12:24. Paul's declaration forced the Pharisees to acknowledge that the followers of Jesus were trying to bear witness to the teaching of the Scriptures.

The fight within the Sanhedrin got out of control and the Roman commander had to intervene to rescue Paul once again. Back in custody, Paul was surrounded by the great powers of state and religion, the powers that had murdered the LORD Jesus.

Jerusalem and Rome were the centres of two enormously strong power blocs. The faith of Jerusalem went back two millennia to Abraham. The rule of Rome extended some three million square miles around the Mediterranean Sea. Jerusalem's strength lay in history and tradition, Rome's in conquest and organization. The combined might of Jerusalem and Rome was overwhelming. If a solitary dissident like Paul were to set himself against them, the outcome would be inevitable. His chances of survival would resemble those of a butterfly before a steamroller. He would be crushed, utterly obliterated from the face off the earth.[106]

Nevertheless, the entire picture changes when we see what happened that very night.

Acts 23:11 – "The following night the Lord stood near Paul and said, "Take courage! As you have testified about me in Jerusalem, so you must also testify in Rome.""

When Jesus is with us we can face anything – even the most powerful empires and corporations in the world. He has promised to stay with His followers even to the end of the world, so whether we live or die, are imprisoned or rejected, yet when Jesus is with us we can face it all.

In prison, Paul knew that above all the powers of this age, Jesus was reigning over the heavens and the earth. Jesus still had work for Paul to do and Paul could continue to speak with courage and respect, without fear.

In the modern age we have become all too familiar with religious, fundamentalist, suicide murderers, yet Paul was the target for 40 of them in the first century. Whenever people put their ideas of truth ahead of grace and love, violence and evil will always follow. Those that follow Jesus will fast from food (and sometimes drink too) in order to draw nearer to Him, to serve others more faithfully, to love with more practical reality, to bring life and hope and justice to those in need. These religious fundamentalists were fasting in order to bring death and terror. Yet, all too many don't care about anything enough to ever fast for any reason!

Were these 40 assassins so devoted to their god that they all died within the week, refusing any food or water, or perhaps the prospect of such a futile death brought them to their senses.

We are filled with questions about Paul's nephew. How was he able to find out about this murder plot? Paul had been tutored under Gamaliel in Jerusalem, so presumably his family was well-connected in the ruling religious families. His families allegiance to the Pharisee party may well have opened

106   John Stott *"The Message of Acts"* – IVP, Leicester, 1990 – page 358.

doors for Paul's nephew so that he overheard this sinister plot. All of these questions fascinate us but we have no definite answers.

The plots at the temple were answered by secretive plots at the Roman garrison. The Roman commander kept the information from Paul's nephew secret and Paul was transferred to Caesarea under an extremely secure guard – 200 soldiers, 200 spearmen and 70 cavalry! It seems clear that the Romans knew how seriously to take threats from religious zealots.

The letter from the Roman commander Claudius Lysias to Governor Felix is broadly accurate, though he does tend to portray himself in the best possible light – verses 25-30. He gives the impression that he rescued Paul from the mob because he already knew that Paul was a Roman citizen. We might speculate that Luke either heard the contents of this letter from Paul or that he may even have seen it for himself.

When Paul got to Herod's palace he was away from the immediate danger of the religious assassins, but he was not set free. He was still kept in prison while his accusers were summoned – verses 31-35.

Men of violence, power and fanaticism surrounded Paul, yet the Sovereign LORD stood with Him and kept Him safe. There may have been plots in the temple and in the garrison, but much more importantly there were divine decisions made in the courts of heaven. Paul was safe in the plans of Jesus.

d. Felix (24:1-27)

It took 5 days for Paul's accuser's to get organised, but eventually the high priest Ananias and a lawyer named Tertullus made their way to Caesarea. Tertullus began with some flattery for Felix who actually had a reputation for cruelty and injustice – verses 1-4.

Paul was accused of being a ringleader of the 'Nazarene sect' or 'Nazarene heresy'(although the word 'heresy' did not yet have the sense of theological deviance that it later had). Jesus had been brought up in the Town of the Nazirites (see Numbers 6), the town were He would have been encouraged in the total dedication that He had to His Father. The fact that His followers had been labelled as the people of His home town shows us how their entire identity was defined by Jesus.

Paul was accused of being three specific things:

1. A troublemaker, stirring up riots among the Jews all over the world;
2. A ringleader of the Nazarene sect;
3. A desecrator of the temple.

Paul carefully defended himself against these three accusations, but began with a more realistic appraisal of Felix – verse 10. Felix would have been most concerned about Paul being a troublemaker stirring up riots, so Paul begins with that. There was no evidence that Paul did anything in Jerusalem other than quietly go to the temple. – verses 11-13. He didn't claim to be a ringleader, but a follower of The Way. Given that Jesus is Himself the Way (John 14:6), this term expresses both the fact that Jesus is the centre and substance of His followers, but also that to follow Him is to obey His teaching and example rather than merely holding to a set of truths.

Yet, this 'Way' was not a recent innovation by Jesus. The Way is nothing more or less than everything that is in the Law and the Prophets – verse 14. Jesus is the very One that Moses and the Prophets were speaking about, as Jesus Himself taught in John 5:39-40. Again aligning himself with the Pharisees on the Sanhedrin, Paul states that the Way of Jesus is exactly what these teachers of the Law should also believe – verses 15-16.

Far from coming to Jerusalem to cause trouble, Paul was actually engaged in humanitarian work, bringing money for the poor – verse 17. He made sure that he was ceremonially clean before he went to the temple – verse 18 – and he didn't bring any mob with him at all.

If anybody had been causing trouble it was the Jews from Asia Minor, probably from Ephesus, who had made the false accusations against Paul. In Roman Law, as in many legal systems, it was very important that the accused is brought face to face with their accuser – see 25:16. Felix knew this and Paul points out that the people who accused him were not present – verse 19. Furthermore, Paul recalls how the Sanhedrin had been unable to find Paul guilty of anything when he stood before them – verse 20.

It was clever of Paul to end his defence by alluding to the fact that the riot that had required Roman intervention was the one caused by the Sanhedrin itself when Paul had mentioned the resurrection – verse 21.

We are told that Felix knew all about the Way of Jesus – verse 22 – so presumably he understood something of the Sanhedrin's track record in relation to Jesus. Paul was guilty of nothing so should have been set free, yet Felix did not want any assassins or riots rampaging around on his watch. Perhaps at a deeper level Felix wanted to hear more about the Way of Jesus – verses 23-25.

However, as Paul explained the Way of Jesus to him, Felix became very uncomfortable – verse 25. It may have been that the talk of self-control had challenged Felix's immoral life (with his desire for bribes – verse 26) or that Felix was terrified of the coming day of Judgement when he would have to answer to the LORD Jesus. However, Paul's discourse of verse 25 may have been a more thorough explanation of the plan of salvation – righteousness; self control and judgement to come.

John Stott points out that this may have been a summary of the past, present and future terms of salvation. We see this in the righteousness that God has given to us in the life, death and resurrection of Jesus in the past; the self-control that the Spirit gives us as we follow Jesus in this present age; the future day of Jesus' return when the wicked will be shut out of His glorious New Creation.

For TWO YEARS Paul was kept in this intolerable situation. From time to time Paul was summoned to speak with Felix, yet the apostle who wanted nothing more than to travel around the Mediterranean world spreading the love, freedom and glory of Jesus was confined in such a futile way.

How could Paul endure this? Do we ever feel that we are also caught in a dead-end, a 'waste of time'? Paul teaches us that beyond all our present frustrations, if we are faithfully following Jesus, then we are safe in the care of our heavenly Father. Paul would do some of his greatest work in prison and these two years of gentle imprisonment (see verse 23) were a vital preparation for the years to come.

e. Paul's appeal to Rome (25:1-12)

When Festus arrived, things began to change – verse 1. Just three days into his administration he investigated Paul's case in Jerusalem. Even after two years the religious leaders were still ready to bring accusations against Paul – verse 2 – and would still like to kill him in Jerusalem – verse 3.

As Felix had done, Festus also convened a court at Caesarea – verses 4-7 – where the religious leaders were still unable to substantiate their accusations against Paul.

Paul's defence against the three accusations was much briefer this time: "I have done nothing wrong against the law of the Jews or against the temple or against Caesar" – verse 8. Festus wanted to begin his governorship by winning over the religious leaders so offered a Jerusalem trial.

Paul had no options left. The religious leaders of Jerusalem were determined to kill him and the new Roman governor did not have the steel of Felix. Paul could see that once he was transferred to Jerusalem, Festus would not be able to keep him safe from the Jewish assassins. In one of the great speeches of human history, Paul the Roman citizen made the ultimate appeal to Caesar himself – verses 10-11. This right was given to Roman citizens to prevent them suffering arbitrary injustice in provincial courts. Paul notes that he was supposed to be in Caesar's court in Caesarea (given that the town was named after the emperor!), yet if the governor could not guarantee the justice of Caesar, then Paul would have to go directly to Caesar.

Paul knew that he had to go to Rome to bear witness to Jesus, as the LORD Himself had promised – 23:11. Paul was less interested in freedom and more interested in being a fruitful, faithful servant of His Master.

Whatever circumstances we face, whatever trouble we are in, whatever conflict surrounds us, the only question we need to answer is 'how can I follow Jesus?' How can I be like Him? How can I lay down my life in service to Jesus and others? How can I forget myself and bring glory to Jesus?

If we are looking for comfort, personal freedom & rights or status & popularity then we will always find our lives wasting away into futility and emptiness. If we trust Jesus, follow His Way and crucify our own desires, then we will always find our lives producing eternal fruit and glory.

Study 9   Bible Questions

Acts 22:30-23:35

1. Verses 30 – What has life been like for Paul since his arrival in Jerusalem? In what ways had his life and habits changed? Why had the commander released Paul and called the Sanhedrin to assemble?

2. Verses 1-5 – What did Paul mean when he stated he had fulfilled his duty to God? Why did this offend the High Priest so much? Why did Paul speak to the High Priest in the way he did?

3. Verses 6-8 – Why did Paul pick on the issue of the resurrection of the dead at this time? What does this say about Paul? What might the modern day equivalent of the Sadducees be?

4. Verses 9-10 – Why was the ensuing dispute so violent? Why did the commander seek to protect Paul from the violence?

5. Verse 11 – How were the Lord's words both an encouragement and a challenge to Paul? How would Paul have felt as a result of what the Lord had said?

6. Verses 12-16 – What does the conspiracy say about the Jews? Why were they so set on killing Paul?

7. Verses 17-22 – How is Paul's life saved on this occasion? What does this say about the way the Lord works out his purposes?

8. Verses 23-30 – How did the commander view the threat by the Jews? What does the fact that the commander sent Paul to the Governor say about the situation?

9. Verses 31-35 – What does Paul's delivery to the Governor say about his message? In what other ways might Paul have been able to speak the truth about Jesus to such a person?

10. Verses 22:30-23:35 – Compare Paul's treatment here with some of the previous encounters he has had as a Christian. What has come of Paul? How is he fulfilling the task God has given him in this situation? How can we do the same?

Study 9   Further Questions

How would you feel about going to a place where you knew you were going to be treated badly, hurt and arrested? What if this treatment were to be purely as a result of the fact that you were a Christian? What words of Jesus might serve as some form of encouragement?

What is the danger of adopting Felix's approach to the gospel message, the approach that says, "When I find it convenient, I will hear more about Jesus"? Who do you know like this? What could you do or say to convince them of the urgency of the matter?

Why was it important for the gospel message to be delivered to Governors, rulers and Kings and not just to the people? What effect has this had on the history of the Christian church?

Study 9   Daily Readings

Day 1	Acts 21
Day 2	Acts 22
Day 3	Acts 23
Day 4	Acts 24
Day 5	Acts 25:1-12
Day 6	Matthew 5:1-12
Day 7	Revelation 19

The daily Bible readings are an opportunity to not only read through all of the material in the book under study, but also to read parts of the Bible that relate to the themes and issues that we have been considering. We try to make sure that we receive light from the whole Bible as we think through the key issues each week.

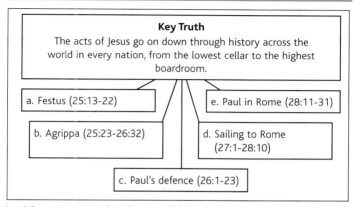

Key Truth
The acts of Jesus go on down through history across the world in every nation, from the lowest cellar to the highest boardroom.

a. Festus (25:13-22)

e. Paul in Rome (28:11-31)

b. Agrippa (25:23-26:32)

d. Sailing to Rome (27:1-28:10)

c. Paul's defence (26:1-23)

It might seem strange that this incredible book that began with a human being ascending to the highest heaven beyond the universe should end with another human being spending years locked up in prison. Surely Luke has made a mistake here! We were gripped and excited by the early stories when the Holy Spirit was visibly present in flames of fire, with earthquakes, foreign languages and miracles. We were inspired when we saw how the Jesus community sold their possessions and began the revolution that would change world history. When we saw how the Kingdom of God was becoming tangible in all the different nations of the world we were amazed by the sovereign power of the Glorified Jesus. Yet, from chapter 21 the scale of history contracts down to this one man who is constantly opposed and thwarted and contained. A quarter of the book seems to happen around court cases and legal defenses.

Why did the Holy Spirit lead Luke to write in this way?

Think of the lives of the prophets, priests and kings through the Hebrew Scriptures. The godly anointed servants of Jesus were misunderstood, rejected and faced continual opposition. Many of them spent years on the run or in prison, weeping, pleading, crying out from the depths. Some were tortured and killed, all in faithful, Spirit-anointed service of the Living God.

The same was true of Jesus Himself. Though filled with joy and peace and glory, yet He was the Man of sorrows, acquainted with grief. To serve Jesus sometimes means excitement but often means suffering and sacrifice. Yes, He will never forsake us and we will often know experiences of His presence that will make us weep with joy and wonder. Yes, we will find Him stand with us when everybody else has abandoned us and His friendship and love will be more than we can endure. Yes, we will know times of refreshing that are filled with unspeakable joy and glory. Yet, to follow Jesus will mean following the very path of sacrifice, service and suffering that He walked before us. We cannot have the love of the world and the love of Jesus. We cannot be popular in both heaven and earth. We cannot store up treasure in both heaven and earth.

The Book of Acts so wonderfully prepares us for the normal Christian life. If the great apostles Paul and Peter spent so much time facing opposition and imprisonment, then we should never be surprised or discouraged when these things happen to us.

Paul spent so much time caught up in legal battles and bureaucratic red tape, yet was so fruitful and faithful to Jesus in it all. For two years he was caught in the world-weary greed and cynicism of Felix's criminal justice system – and yet the Way of Jesus was lived and spoken right there in Caesarea.

We may feel that all the legal battles and bureaucratic time wasting prevent us from serving Jesus, from advancing the kingdom, from bearing eternal fruit. Praise God that His Word shows us the great global apostle caught up in all the same frustrations that we face.

If the book of Acts ended with an explosion of Pentecostal miracles with fire and earthquakes, then we would always wonder why that story ended so long ago. Yet, precisely because the book of Acts ends with a man struggling to bear witness to Jesus in a tangle of legal and bureaucratic frustrations, we know that this story is still going on all over the world today. This story is our story. The Word of God prepares us for the frustrations and challenges of normal life in this present darkness – with all the wonderful providence of our Living LORD Jesus who never forsakes us.

a. Festus (25:13-22)

Before Paul could be sent to Rome another defence had to be made. King Agrippa and Bernice arrived to wish Festus well on his new appointment, but while they were there Festus wanted the advice of somebody who understood not only the intricacies of Jewish theology but also how that might relate to Roman law.

As Festus explains the situation to Agrippa we get a sense of his confusion.

He had walked into a mess that Felix left him and he was clearly NOT as well-acquainted with the Way as Felix had been. He was expecting Paul to be accused of normal crimes that Roman law recognised, yet – verse 19 – his accusers "had some points of dispute with (Paul) about their own religion and about a dead man named Jesus whom Paul claimed was alive. I was at a loss how to investigate such matters…"

b. Agrippa (25:23-26:32)

Agrippa wanted to hear more from Paul and we are told that when Agrippa arrived at the hearing he was accompanied by Bernice – "with great pomp" (verse 23). With them came a selection of local celebrities and Festus used the opportunity to make a rather dramatic speech to the assembled audience – verses 24-27. Festus claimed that he had nothing to write to Caesar (verse 26) and yet he had heard the charges from the Jerusalem Jewish leaders.

It is said that Bernice was not only Agrippa's twin sister but had earlier been married to a son of the brother of the great Bible scholar Philo from Alexandria. Philo may well have been the greatest Bible student of all history and his ability to take the greatest findings of Scriptural scholarship and present them to the wider Greek speaking world was an incredible achievement. Philo understood that the Law of Moses looked forward to a Divine Messiah who would be the Great High Priest of the whole cosmos. Philo dives deep into the Hebrew understanding of the Trinity before any of the New Testament had been written.

If Philo had been the uncle of Bernice's husband, then we can understand that Agrippa might well have been very well-informed about the deep truths of the Hebrew Scriptures. It is perhaps for this reason that Paul acknowledges Agrippa's depth of theological and Scriptural learning – 26:3, 26-27 – even if Agrippa did not have the corresponding godliness.

It was a dramatic moment when the holy and humble apostle of Jesus Christ stood before this representative of the worldly, ambitious, morally corrupt family of the Herods, who for generation after generation had set themselves in opposition to truth and righteousness. 'Their founder, Herod the Great', wrote R. B. Rackham, 'had tried to destroy the infant Jesus. His son Antipas, the tetrarch of Galilee, beheaded John the Baptist, and won from the Lord the title of 'fox'. His grandson Agrippa I slew James the son of Zebedee with the sword. Now we see Paul brought before Agrippa's son'.[107]

c. Paul's defence (26:1-23)

In Acts 12:17; 13:16 and 26:1 Paul 'motioned with his hand' as he began to address his audience. It is a small detail that helps us to get a glimpse of this short man who was able to bear so much eternal fruit to the glory of Jesus.

Once again Paul told his biography, but over the previous two years he had learned to give his testimony with more focus and purpose. In 22:6 he had described his Damascus road experience as "a bright light from heaven flashed around me", but now he spoke of "a light from heaven, brighter than the sun, blazing around me and my companions."

Paul's defense was split into four sections:

1. A devoted Pharisee   (verses 4-8)
2. Zealous against Jesus   (verses 9-11)
3. Commissioned by Jesus   (verses 12-18)
4. Faithfully serving Jesus   (verses 19-23)

1. A devoted Pharisee   (verses 4-8)
Paul was well known, since childhood, as a strict member of the Pharisee sect. No one could question his devotion to the Scriptures and the great hope of Israel, the resurrection of the dead.

2. Zealous against Jesus   (verses 9-11)
Paul had initially been fiercely opposed to Jesus of Nazareth and with great zeal did all he could to imprison and murder His followers. He travelled around synagogues stirring up trouble against the followers of Way.

---

107 Stott, page 370.

3. Commissioned by Jesus   (verses 12-18)

However, whilst on such a mission, Jesus appeared to him from heaven and spoke to him in Aramaic, revealing that Paul's opposition to the Christians put him in opposition to the LORD Himself. The LORD Jesus gave Paul a new mission in life – verses 17 – "I will rescue you from your own people and from the Gentiles. I am sending you to them to open their eyes and turn them from darkness to light, and from the power of Satan to God."

It is very important to note how this commissioning of Paul is just like the commissioning of Moses (Exodus 3:1-6) or Isaiah (Isaiah 6:1-13) or especially Ezekiel (Ezekiel 1:1-3:15). Ezekiel had also encountered the divine glory of the Son of Man (Ezekiel 1:25-28) and was also commissioned to serve Him in the international arena.

We are supposed to see how Moses, Ezekiel, Paul and Isaiah are all equally servants of Jesus. Each of them was personally commissioned by Him and each faced a life of opposition and suffering, a life of preaching to an unresponsive Israel.

4. Faithfully serving Jesus   (verses 19-23)

Commissioned by the LORD God of the prophets, Paul could not be disobedient to this heavenly vision – verse 19. He carried on with his wide travels but now to tell both Jews and foreigners to turn around towards the Living God, proving this repentance in practical action. The Way of Jesus is not a new idea, but is the same faith of Israel that has been taught in the Law and the Prophets since the very beginning.

It was crucial that the Way of Jesus was understood to be the original message of the Law and the Prophets. If Jesus had brought a new message, something that had never been intended by Moses and the Prophets, then the teachers of the Law would have been quite right to oppose Him. The reason that Paul and the other apostles spend so much time explaining the original meaning of Moses and the Prophets is to demonstrate from Scripture that Jesus is the Promised Messiah.

Verses 22-23 state this in one of Paul's most powerful theological statements – "I stand here and testify to small and great alike. I am saying nothing beyond what the prophets and Moses said would happen – that the Christ would suffer and, as the first to rise from the dead, would proclaim light to His own people and to the Gentiles."

Paul's summary of the teaching of the Hebrew Scriptures is so similar to Jesus' own summary in Luke 24:44-47.

> (Jesus) said to them, "This is what I told you while I was still with you: Everything must be fulfilled that is written about me in the Law of Moses, the Prophets and the Psalms." Then he opened their minds so they could understand the Scriptures. He told them, "This is what is written: The Christ will suffer and rise from the dead on the third day, and repentance and forgiveness of sins will be preached in his name to all nations, beginning at Jerusalem.

It is vitally important that we take this seriously for ourselves. As we read through the Hebrew Scriptures, are we arriving at this conclusion?

Do we see how Jesus is the main character in both the Old and the New Testament? How does the Law of Moses teach that Jesus had to suffer?

Where do the Hebrew Scriptures teach about Jesus rising from the dead? How would we show people how salvation was always for both Jews and foreigners?

If Paul's entire message and theology was nothing more than the message and theology of Moses and the Prophets, we need such a deep sense of the message and theology of the Bible. The gospel of Jesus is not a new idea or something that only emerged in the middle of history.

The gospel has always been the same from the beginning of the world to the end of the world. Salvation has only ever been through trusting Jesus, whether those saints who looked forward to His birth, life, death and resurrection or those of us who look back to His saving work.

The 39 articles of the Church of England have a wonderful statement of this:

VII.   Of the Old Testament.
The Old Testament is not contrary to the New: for both in the Old and New Testament everlasting life is offered to Mankind by Christ, who is the only Mediator between God and Man, being both God and Man. Wherefore they are not to be heard, which feign that the old Fathers did look only for transitory promises.

Festus found it all insane – verses 24-25. Yet, Paul knew that Agrippa had a deeper knowledge of these things. All that had happened to Jesus was done in the public domain and it was common knowledge – verse 26. Paul put the challenge directly: if Agrippa believed in the prophets then he must also trust in Jesus – verse 27.

Though Agrippa refused to accept salvation so quickly – verse 28 – yet he acknowledged that Paul had done nothing wrong – verse 31.

d. Sailing to Rome (27:1-28:10)

We have enjoyed such a detailed account of the events of Paul's trial and defence we suspect that Luke himself must have been close at hand and our suspicions are confirmed when we read in Acts 27:1 that Luke travelled with Paul to Rome. Julius, the centurion, was placed in charge of the journey (verse 1) and they sailed along the northern coast of the Mediterranean with Aristarchus, who had joined Paul back in Acts 20:4.

Paul was allowed limited freedom so he was able to meet up with churches along the journey – verse 3. Luke's careful description of the daily travels on board the ship indicates that he kept a daily log of the journey. The weather was unfavourable and although they found an Alexandrian ship taking grain to Rome (verse 6 & 38), yet they made very slow progress, being forced off course towards Crete (verse 7).

Paul was obviously a seasoned maritime traveler and advised that the journey be postponed until the weather improved (verse 9-10). However, the pilot and ship's owner were driven by the need to realise some profit on the grain cargo and decided to keep going – verses 11-12. However, as they sailed along the coast of Crete a hurricane force wind (verse 14) drove them off course and into serious danger. They had to begin get rid of the cargo and ship's tackle (verses 18-19).

For many days they were held in the darkness of this ferocious storm, without any hope – verse 20.

So people find it very strange that Paul the academic and leatherworker should have more understanding of the sea than the professional sailors, yet there is more going on here than mere maritime skills.

Throughout the Bible the sea has a much deeper meaning.

Right from Genesis 1:2 the sea is a place of chaos and darkness. The land had to be divided away from the sea (Genesis 1:9-10) even as the light had to be divided from the darkness (Genesis 1:3-5). The sea represents the Abyss (The Deep) – the pit of darkness and chaos that contains all that is opposed to the Living God.

When the judgement of the LORD God destroyed the ancient world the sea was allowed to overwhelm the whole land – Genesis 6-8. Jeremiah laments that the great sin of Israel is like the sea (Lamentations 2:13). Isaiah sees how the wicked are like the sea – "But the wicked are like the tossing sea, which cannot rest, whose waves cast up mire and mud. 'There is no peace," says my God, "for the wicked'" (Isaiah 57:20-21). Yet, the LORD would stay with Jesus even when He is on the sea – Isaiah 43:2.

The fact that the Angel of the LORD was able to divide the Red Sea so that the people of Israel could pass through on dry ground is seen as one of the most amazing miracles in the whole Bible. His sovereignty over the sea in the book of Jonah also reveals His mighty power.

We see this same truth most fully in the biographies of Jesus. The winds and waves actually obey Jesus, which the disciples find completely terrifying – Mark 4:35-41. The fact that Jesus' control of the sea is followed by His control over the demons (Mark 5:1-20) is no accident. The same LORD who can command even the chaos of the sea is surely able to command the chaos of the evil spirits.

> Psalm 89:9-10 – "O LORD God Almighty, who is like you? You are mighty, O LORD, and your faithfulness surrounds you. You rule over the surging sea; when its waves mount up, you still them."

Jesus is able to walk on the sea – Mark 6:45-51 – which also terrified the disciples. Power over the sea, in Biblical terms, is the greatest power of all. Job 9:8 tells us that the LORD God "alone stretches out the heavens and treads on the waves of the sea."

Ezekiel looked forward to the new creation when the sea would be replaced by fresh water – 47:1-12. This vision is confirmed by John in Revelation 21:1 – "Then I saw a new heaven and a new earth, for the first heaven and the first earth had passed away, and there was no longer any sea."

With all this in mind we need to read these chapters of Acts with a deeper Biblical awareness. Paul's calm authority in the face of the terrifying darkness of the storm is showing us how Paul was completely identified with his LORD, Jesus. Just as both Paul and Jesus resolutely set their faces to Jerusalem knowing what awaited them there, just as they faced the trials of the Jewish and Roman courts, just as the Jews had called for the death of them both, so Paul was allowed to share in Jesus' mastery over the sea.

When all hope of salvation was gone (Acts 27:20), Paul was able to give the impossible guarantee of total safety that only the Living God could bring (verses 21-26). In verse 23, Jesus Himself came to Paul and stood with him yet again in the darkness and chaos. The same promise Jesus gave to Paul in the depths of the prison in Acts 23:11, was repeated to him again with the further gracious promise of safety for everybody on the ship.

Just as we saw Paul sustained by Jesus through the chaos and darkness of prison and persecution, this same truth is played out by His care for Paul through the sea and the storm.

If Jesus is with us, then we need have no fear of the chaos and darkness of this world, no matter how fierce it may seem. Jesus has all the power and authority to deliver us safely just as He wills.

In Acts 27:27-44 Luke shows us the amazing way that Jesus' apostle was able to bring salvation to the entire crew – so long as they paid careful attention to his instructions. As Paul broke bread for the entire ship's company (verse 35), so the whole company was bound together and all were delivered.

The LORD Jesus had landed them safely on Malta and they received unusual kindness from the islanders – 28:1-2

However, as Paul gathered firewood he was bitten by a snake – verse 3. This also sends us back to the Hebrew Scriptures. In Genesis chapter 3 the ancient serpent led humanity into exile from the Living God. Yet, even then, in Genesis 3:15, we are told of the coming of Jesus who would crush the snake. In Exodus 4:1-5 Moses was given something of this authority over the serpent as he went to face Pharaoh. In Romans 16:20 Paul himself notes how this authority over Satan is given to the followers of Jesus. As Paul threw the snake into the fire, so Luke is giving us a symbolic presentation of the way the church of Jesus will not only triumph over Satan but will finally judge him – see Luke 10:1-20.

The Maltese people recognise the theological significance of the snake bite — verse 4 & 6. In verse 4 they see that such a snake bite must reveal Paul's evil nature, however when Paul is able to cast the snake into the fire without any harm, they recognise that such power and authority is a sign of divinity.

Throughout these chapters we are shown how Paul is so closely identified with Jesus especially when Paul is going through such hardship, opposition and suffering. This goes even further in verses 7-10. The healing power of the Spirit of Jesus was given to Paul so that he was able to heal all the sick that were brought to him. Luke writes a scene that creates deep echoes with his biography of Jesus — Luke 4:38-40.[108]

e. Paul in Rome (28:11-31)

It was three months before they were able to continue the voyage and Luke notes how the Alexandrian boat was trusting its safety to the twin gods Castor and Pollux — verse 11 — even though these gods had showed no ability to protect anybody earlier on the journey.

News of Paul's approach to Rome had spread among the local Christians and they came to meet him as he completed the journey on land — verses 14-16. Paul was especially grateful for this wonderful fellowship — verse 15.

In Rome Paul was kept under guard, but it was clearly the kind of 'gentle' imprisonment that he had been allowed in Caesarea — verse 16.

Paul was worried that rumours may have circulated against him over the previous three years. It was clearly very important for him to set the record straight, so he called the Jewish leaders together to give yet another defence of his service to the LORD God of Israel.

Summarising what had happened to me and explaining how he was innocent of all accusations, Paul stated that was "because of the hope of Israel that I am bound with this chain" (verse 20).

> Paul had done nothing against the Jews, the Romans had nothing against him, and he had nothing (i.e. no charge) against the Jews. It was in order to clarify these points that he had asked to see them.

---

108 What are we to make of the fact that all the time periods in this account are in threes? Three days in 28:7; three months in 28:11; three days 28:12; and three days in 28:17.

He was a loyal Jew; indeed it was because of the hope of Israel, Israel's Messianic expectation fulfilled in Jesus, that he was a prisoner.[109]

The Jewish leaders had heard nothing about Paul, but had heard much about the Way of Jesus and were eager for Paul's understanding of it – verses 21-22.

Luke does not record the specific arguments and Biblical explanations that Paul set before these Jewish leaders in verse 23. However, he does tell us that the heart of Paul's argument was based on showing how Moses and the Prophets were speaking about Jesus the Promised Messiah. If we consider all that Paul writes in his letters we could build up a good idea of what he spoke about and the specific Scriptures that he would have chosen.

How would we do this? What aspects of Moses writings would we choose?

What prophecies reveal the identity and mission of Jesus most clearly?

Paul's gospel presentation divided the Jewish audience. Some were ready to believe the Scriptures and accept Jesus, whereas others rejected their Messiah – verse 24. Paul didn't want the day to end with a vague sense of indecision, so he concluded his argument with a very direct challenge, quoting from Isaiah 6:9-10.

We noted how Paul's own commissioning from Jesus was so similar to the way that the LORD Jesus had commissioned Moses, Isaiah and Ezekiel. Paul chose the commissioning of Isaiah to explain the urgency of his own message to them. Just as Isaiah had encountered hard-hearted unbelief and opposition from Israel in his own day, so Paul was facing the same thing. Acts 28:25-28.

The Holy Spirit spoke the truth to your forefathers when he said through Isaiah the prophet: "Go to this people and say,
You will be ever hearing but never understanding;
you will be ever seeing but never perceiving.
For this people's heart has become calloused;
they hardly hear with their ears, and they have closed their eyes.
Otherwise they might see with their eyes, hear with their ears,
understand with their hearts and turn, and I would heal them."

Therefore I want you to know that God's salvation has been sent to the Gentiles, and they will listen!

---

109   Stott, page 398

The prophecy of Isaiah is full of predictions of how the kingdom of God would spread far beyond the limits of the land of Israel to all the nations of the world – Isaiah 11:10; 42:6; 49:6 etc. The Jewish people of Paul's day were experiencing the fulfilment of these mighty prophecies and they needed to repent and believe in their LORD God who was going on ahead of them to the whole world.

The glorious LORD Jesus who ascended to the highest heaven is the LORD God of the whole earth. His kingdom cuts across all the barriers of this present darkness, bringing love, justice and truth to peoples who have been lost in greed, fear, materialism, religion and despair. Every language, every tribe, every culture is welcomed into the wonderful Kingdom of Jesus. Just like the ancient people we too might prefer our own comfortable 'religion' to the Jesus Revolution, but then we too will be blind and deaf even though we might be surrounded by Biblical truth.

Paul was able to rent his own house in Rome (verse 30) and he welcomed "all who came to see him". Notice how there is no longer any reference to Jew or Gentile. Paul's service in Rome was to all people regardless of their religious background or genetic heritage. If he had spent two years in limited ministry in Felix's prison, here under Caesar's guard he was able to speak about Jesus without hindrance – verse 31.

Paul's letter from this Roman imprisonment to the Philippians reveals something of Paul's success in bearing witness to Jesus – Philippians 4:22 – "All the saints send you greetings, especially those who belong to Caesar's household."

How are we using our own situation?

It is all too easy to spend our time complaining about our circumstances, wishing and praying that our circumstances would be more suited to our own desires. Grumbling is one of the most terrible spiritual diseases that we can ever develop and once it is within us it is extremely hard to root out.

If we have been inspired and challenged by these continuing acts of Jesus by His Spirit through His servants, then we must see how Luke has directed our lesson. In all our frustrations and opposition, with all our weaknesses and burdens, with all the time pressures and lack of support, yet if we look to Jesus He will never abandon us and He will surely continue His acts even through us until all the kingdoms of this world become His kingdom.

Study 10   Bible Questions

Acts 28:11-31

1. Verses 11-14 – What had the journey to Rome been like for Paul and his companions? What does this say about the significance of his visit there? What would it have been like for Paul to stay for a week with believers in Puteoli?

2. Verses 15-16 – How had the gospel reached Rome prior to Paul arriving there? What does this say abut the spread of the gospel? Why was Paul allowed to live by himself with only a soldier to guard him?

3. Verses 17-18 – Why did Paul persist in speaking to the Jewish leaders? How does Paul explain his innocence?

4. Verses 19-20 – On what grounds does Paul say he is due to appear before Caesar? Why does Paul think he is in chains at this time?

5. Verses 21-22 – Why did the Jews of Jerusalem not write to the Jews in Rome to warn them against Paul? How do the Jewish leaders in Rome describe the gospel message?

6. Verses 23-24 – What does the attendance at the meeting say about the mission field in front of Paul? What two aspects did Paul focus on in his teaching?

7. Verses 25-28 – Why did some of the people leave at this point? Why did some people find it so hard to believe Paul? How did Paul end his speech and what are the implications of this?

8. Verses 30-31 – What does we find Paul doing at the end of this book and why? How is he being treated by his captors? What does this say?

9. Verses 11-31 – Paul's life to this point has been a real struggle yet he seems at last to have arrived at one of his goals. What else does Paul do during these two years of proclaiming the gospel? Why does Acts end here? Where do we fit in?

BookbyBook

Study 10   Further Questions

What place does the sea and in particular storms at sea play in Biblical thought? See for example passages such as Genesis 1:1-10, Jeremiah 5:22, Mark 4:34-41, Revelation 21:1. What should our attitude be towards the sea?

What are the similarities between the trial of Jesus and the trials of Paul? What are the differences? What does this tell us about the way Jesus' followers can expect to be treated?

Why was it so important for Paul to reach Rome? It appears that there was already a group of believers in this city as he had written to them prior to his visit (Romans 1:11, 15:23-33), so why was he so anxious to visit there himself? Are there any modern day equivalents of this journey to Rome?

Study 10   Daily Readings

Day 1	Acts 25:13-27
Day 2	Acts 26
Day 3	Acts 27
Day 4	Acts 28
Day 5	Romans 1
Day 6	2 Corinthians 11:16-33
Day 7	Revelation 7:9-17

The daily Bible readings are an opportunity to not only read through all of the material in the book under study, but also to read parts of the Bible that relate to the themes and issues that we have been considering. We try to make sure that we receive light from the whole Bible as we think through the key issues each week.

Suggested Answers to the Bible Study Questions

Acts 1:1-11

1. Verse 1 – Both books are written to the same person and Jesus is the main player in both. However Luke tells us at the beginning of Acts that his first book was about all that Jesus "began" to do and teach. This second book therefore is about what Jesus continued to do and teach.

2. Verses 2-3 – Jesus wanted to teach them about his resurrection after it had happened, when it was easier for his followers to understand what had happened and what it meant. Furthermore, Jesus wanted to show his followers what resurrection life looked at. This gives us a glimpse of what life will we be like when, on Resurrection Morning, we receive our news bodies, because they will be like his resurrection body (1 John 3:2).

3. Verses 4-5 – It was right and fitting and biblical that this message should begin in Jerusalem, the place that had been the centre of all God's purposes for many hundreds of years, and also the very place where the Lord of this life was murdered. The Holy Spirit was promised by God the Father in many places in the Old Testament, but also promised and spoken of by Jesus throughout his teaching. The Spirit seems to be sent by the Father and the Son.

4. Verse 6 – Their vision was far too small and centred on Israel alone. The mission Jesus was just about to detail again for them was on a scale they hadn't yet imagined. Their question might appear reasonable on the face of it however they hadn't read and understood that this restoration was not going to be limited to Israel, but would affect the whole world.

5. Verses 7-8 – In one respect, being a witness to Jesus is quite straightforward. Telling people about who Jesus is and what he has achieved is not a complicated message. Jesus opens their eyes and helps them to see the vision for the world that he and his Father have.

6. Verse 9 – Jesus needed to take his rightful place at the side of the Father in the throne room of heaven (Mark 16:19, Ephesians 4:8-10) so this is one reason why he had to leave. Jesus had to depart from his friends and there had to be a very public and clear act of ascension on the part of Jesus to ensure that his followers knew, not only that he had left but also where he had gone to.

7. Verses 10-11 – How could a person just be lifted up off the ground and travel straight up into the sky? The resurrection truly was a remarkable event as Jesus had predicted it would be in John 6:60-62.

8. Verses 1-11 – Like the apostles, we too are waiting for Jesus to return and in the meantime, we are given the great commission of Matthew 28:18-20. We too need the help of the Holy Spirit in order to carry out our task.

Acts 2:1-13

1. Verse 1 – This Feast was the feast signifying completion and arrival. Exodus 23:16. It was also the only feast where a believer was allowed to eat bread with yeast in it, signifying that there was time, because the work of redemption was complete and union with the Living God was accomplished.

2. Verse 2 – There is one Hebrew word for breath, and spirit and wind. The Holy Spirit is often seen as both wind and breath. See for example Genesis 2:7 and Ezekiel 37:9-14. The fact that the sound was like a "violent" wind and not a gentle breeze meant that Holy Spirit was up to the enormous task that lay ahead.

3. Verse 3 – The fact that the Spirit could be seen resting on each of them individually, meant they were all as individuals, given the task of proclaiming the greatness of God to those around about them. The Holy Spirit is often associated with fire and this seems to speak of purity and cleansing. See also Isaiah 4:4, Matthew 3:11.

4. Verse 4 – As each believer is filled with the Holy Spirit, they begin to speak. The Spirit is given to equip a believer for a task and more often than not, that task is the task of speaking to other people about Jesus.

5. Verse 5 – At this stage it is important to note that the people who were present were all Jews. The fact that they had come from so many different parts of the world demonstrated that this message was not a local or parochial message. Each of these people would return home within a few days and then they themselves would tell their friends and neighbours about what they had seen and heard.

6. Verses 6-8 – The fact that these people were praising God in the native language of people from every nation under heaven was truly astonishing. Could there have been any better gift for the Holy Spirit to give the followers of Jesus than this gift at this time?

7. Verses 9-11 – Throughout the Bible, these nations had been enemies of the people of God, often taking God's people captive or attacking and defeating them. Therefore the message of this new life was going to reach even these places

8. Verse 13 – The hardness of the hearts of some people and their disinterest with matters relating to God will always amaze. When Jesus was crucified, once again we read of those who mocked and who missed the point completely. Mark 15:16-20, 31-32.

9. Verses 1-13 – The most obvious meaning of these strange and powerful events is that the message of Jesus, to which these men were bearing witness, was a message for all the nations of the earth. The events described here mark a reversal of the events at the Tower of Babel described in Genesis 11:1-9. The gift of languages should be of great benefit and be a necessity in our churches if they are the multinational and multilingual collection of people coming together to praise God and declare his greatness.

Acts 4:1-22

1. Verses 1-2 – It was the fact that the apostles were proclaiming in Jesus the resurrection of the dead that bothered the religious leaders so much. It was bad enough that one person had apparently been raised from the dead, let alone that Resurrection Morning was approaching.

2. Verses 3-4 – The fact that those who delivered the message had been arrested and put in prison didn't seem to put people off because the message was about matters of eternal significance.

3. Verses 5-6 – In John 18:12-14 we read that Caiaphas and Annas oversaw the farcical trial of Jesus in the early hours of Good Friday morning. Now, a few weeks later, the same men are overseeing this encounter with two of his followers.

4. Verse 7 – Presumably they were looking to try and expose Peter and John as disciples of the Devil. So angered and jealous were they that they didn't seem to spend a moment contemplating the wonder of the miracle itself.

5. Verse 8 – This is the second time that Peter is filled with the Holy Spirit (see also Acts 2:4) and it happens once again in 4:31. On each occasion the Spirit fills Peter to enable him to speak the truth about Jesus.

6. Verse 9 – Peter describes what happened as an act of kindness shown to a cripple. Peter and John are engaged in the Kingdom work that Jesus himself had engaged in (Luke 13:10-17) and had taught his followers to copy (Luke 9:1-2).

7. Verses 10-11 – He accuses not only the people of Israel, but also the very men seated in front of him of the murder of the Son of God. Peter was clearly not delivering a speech that was aimed at securing his safe release and gaining the favour of his accusers. Rather he was taking the opportunity to speak the truth about Jesus and calling people to repent and seek forgiveness.

8. Verses 12 – To claim that salvation could be found in the one crucified as a criminal in this very city a few weeks previously would have been a bold enough statement. However Peter insists that salvation can only be found in this person. Furthermore, Peter doesn't only claim that salvation can be found in this name, but insists that salvation must be found in this name.

9. Verses 13-17 – They were ordinary men given great courage because they had been with Jesus. They had spent time with him and had followed him learnt his ways and committed to live as he lived. This must be our aim also. The fact that the religious leaders concluded that an "outstanding miracle" had been carried out in front of them seemed not to bother them at all. Still their eyes remained blind to the truth

10. Verses 18-22 – Whilst the religious leaders can't decide what to do about it all, the people were praising God for what had happened. The life of Jesus lived and spoken about causes such clear and deep divisions

11. Verses 1-22 – Peter gives us guidance in terms of both the content of the message we should proclaim, the clarity and directness we might need to use on some occasions and the commitment to the message, despite the cost to himself.

Acts 6:12-15 and 7:44-60

1. Verses 12-15 – In chapter 2, some people mocked. In chapter 4 Peter and John are arrested. In chapter 5 the opposition has increased to physical attacks and floggings and in chapter 6, we see internal strife and division. Now the opposition reaches arrest and trial and ultimately murder.

2. Verses 44-46 – The tabernacle was made in accordance with the pattern given to Moses in the desert. Thus it was not a man made attempt to approach the Living God, but God's way of representing reality to his people in a massive visual aid. The fact that the tabernacle moved with the people when the people moved, demonstrated that the God who was served at the tabernacle also moved with his people; he wanted to be where they were, always in their midst.

3. Verses 47-50 – Solomon's temple was a truly magnificent structure. If anything was a suitable earthly representation of the God who was served in the Temple, then surely a building such as this was. Furthermore, the Living God of Heaven had stated that his Name and his eyes and his heart would be there at the Temple forever. Stephen shows his accusers that there is little more serious than focussing more on the temple than on the God that the Temple was meant to represent because by doing so, they eventually rejected God.

4. Verses 51-53 – By disobeying what was written and by deliberately focussing on the form and place of worship instead of the person to be worshipped and in rejecting Jesus, the one ultimately filled with the Holy Spirit in absolute fullness, Stephen's accusers were resisting the Holy Spirit.

5. Verse 54 – The crowds of people in Jerusalem were cut to the heart as Peter exposed their sin and unbelief and many repented and were born again into the family of God

6. Verses 55-56 – Stephen sees the risen Lord Jesus, no longer seated at the right hand of the Father, but standing, ready to receive the soul of his martyr Stephen. His accusers are convinced that Stephen is blaspheming. We too can be encouraged to know that Jesus is never far from us and he is especially close and actively involved at the times when we suffer for him.

7. Verses 57-58 – The so called leaders of God's people have turned into animals who are intent on violent murder. Saul was involved in this violent murder, not only seeing what happened, but assisting those who carried it out. Luke would have us know that Saul was truly on the very extreme end of those who persecuted Jesus' followers, in order to help us appreciate the transformation that was about to follow.

8. Verses 59-60 – Jesus prayed for the forgiveness of those who unjustly killed him, as Stephen does. Jesus was killed at the hands of those in authority who should have known better, just as Stephen was. For the believer, death is like falling asleep. See for example 1 Thessalonians 4:13.

9. Verses 44-60 – As we have already noticed, Stephen considered the gospel message to be of greater importance than his own physical safety.

Acts 9:1-31

1. Verses 1-2 – Saul was still very much of the mind he was in when we last met him in 8:3. The fact that he was prepared to travel from Jerusalem to Damascus was a sign of the zeal with which he went about this task. There seems little doubt that at this stage of his life that Saul had little regard for Jesus and considered him to be anything but the Messiah, God the Son.

2. Verses 3-6 – Jesus' words show his wonderfully close association with his church. Furthermore, Jesus' words in verse 6 indicate that Jesus was not simply seeking to put a stop to the persecution in Damascus.

3. Verses 7-9 – It is possible that their hearts remained hardened to the voice of the ascended Lord and certainly this was a message aimed directly at Saul.

4. These three days would surely have been a clear sign to Saul that, although he had previously thought he could see everything clearly and was in charge of his own destiny, now he needed to know that he had previously been blind to the truth.

5. Verses 10-16 – The church in Damascus had clearly heard lots about Saul and were anticipating the arrival of this zealous, violent man, presumably with great fear. To be told to go out and meet him, and declare that you are one of the people he has come to find, would have been the equivalent of suicide

6. Verses 17-19 – Ananias believed and trusted in Jesus and what Jesus said to him. Presumably Saul regains his sight at the point at which he sees and understands that the very people who he has been seeking to destroy are the ones he needs to trust and protect. Only now has Saul begun to see things clearly.

7. Verses 20-22 – Saul went immediately into the synagogues, to the Jews and began telling them that Jesus was the Son of God. In response, many of the Jews in the synagogues were "baffled".

8. Verses 23-25 – Having such a zealous and learned man against them clearly caused great concern for the Jews. They needed to be rid of him and soon, or he could really make a difference. Saul had a very early taste of the new way of life he would follow here in Damascus.

9. Verses 26-30 – Quite understandably the believers in Jerusalem are afraid of Saul for the reasons set out above. Yet as he continues to speak boldly about Jesus, the believers eventually come round. This must have been a wonderfully exciting realisation for the Jerusalem disciples. If Jesus could transform this frightening and hard man, he could transform anyone. Barnabas presumably believed not only what Saul said, but also saw the difference in his life.

10. Verse 31 – There is now a church in Judea, in Galilee and in Samaria. The first part of the commission that Jesus had given his disciples had been fulfilled. This verse intentionally leaves us on the precipice of the next phase in the march of the gospel.

11. Verses 1-31 – Clearly Saul's conversion was a dramatic event and one in which Jesus very obviously takes the initiative. Saul was chosen for a very special mission and without this direct and face to face encounter with the risen Lord Jesus, it is difficult to imagine how Saul could have carried out the work he was called to.

Acts 14:1-20

1. Verses 1-2 – This method of Paul and Barnabas mirrors the pattern that Jesus gave his followers at the beginning of the book (1:8) and the pattern that Peter recognised in 3:26. See also Romans 1:16. The Jews' hostility is born out of jealousy and because their special status as the chosen people of God was being threatened.

2. Verses 3-7 – Despite, or perhaps because of the opposition they faced, Paul and Barnabas spent considerable time there. They didn't see opposition and attack and plans to kill them as failure. In response, the risen Lord Jesus enabled them to perform signs and wonders in this place that drew the attention of the people. When signs and wonders become the message or distract from the message, they are no longer achieving their purpose.

3. Verses 1-7 – People of radically different backgrounds and even sworn enemies can be united as a result of the gospel, both in a positive way and in a negative way. At Iconium, Jews and Gentiles are united both in their commitment (v1) and their opposition to the gospel (v 5).

4. Verses 8-10 – This incident is reminiscent of the healing carried out by Peter in chapter 3 at the Beautiful Gate in Jerusalem. There Peter specifically says, "in the name of Jesus Christ of Nazareth, walk". Here, Paul merely calls out and tells this crippled person to stand up.

5. Verses 11-13 – Anyone who can bring about such an instant and powerful miracle must be worthy of some attention and perhaps even worthy to be worshipped. Their actions indicate that in this city the dominant religious view was not Jewish but pagan, which is confirmed by the fact that the priest present was from the Temple of Zeus.

6. Verses 14-18 – In Paul's speech in the previous chapter he is in a synagogue in Pisidian Antioch and therefore addressing Jewish people who knew the scriptures. As a result, he quotes a number of times from the Old Testament and mentions significant Old Testament characters. Here in Lystra, these people would not have known their Old Testament so the method and style of preaching were different, however, the message itself remained similar.

7. Verses 19-20 – The fickleness of the crowds in Lystra is noticeable. However, even at what appears to be a very early stage in the work of these two godly witnesses, there was a church in Lystra and the believers gathered round Paul and helped him up and restored him. The fact that Paul went back into the city he had just been so violently ejected from demonstrates once again his lack of concern for his own safety.

8. Verses 1-20 – There is nothing to indicate there was a single believer in either of these two cities at the start of this chapter, yet by the end there is a group of disciples in both. This is what happens when people spread the good news about Jesus without counting the cost to themselves.

Acts 16:11-40

1. Verses 11-12 – According to the previous verses, Paul and his companions found their hopes and plans changed by the Spirit of Jesus. Knowing that this was the region that the Lord wanted them to visit Paul heads for the capital, the place where the gospel could have the biggest audience and the most significant impact.

2. Verses 13-15 – Here in Philippi however, there does not appear to be a synagogue but this doesn't deter Paul. Paul begins chatting about Jesus to some of the women, not a public address to large crowds, but a one to one or a small group discussion. For all that Paul said, we are reminded that it was the Lord that opened Lydia's heart.

3. Verses 16-18 – The ability to predict something about the future doesn't happen by accident, but by the power of Satan and the occult. This was not welcome assistance for Paul but an unhelpful hindrance and distraction to the gospel work.

4. Verses 19-21 – The masters of this slave girl, who are only interested in the money they can make, think nothing of the change of life in this poor slave girl and appear to accept nothing of what Paul and his companions are saying. Perhaps the visit to Philippi had a much greater influence than just Lydia and the jailor.

5. Verses 22-24 – There was no trial, merely the accusations made by the owners of the slave girl and the shouting of the mob. Bleeding and in immense pain, exhausted and probably in shock, Paul and Silas could hardly fall asleep, but they would surely have been forgiven for just keeping quiet and waiting until they could escape from this dreadful place.

6. Verses 25-26 – Even here, they couldn't stop thinking about, talking to and singing to their Jesus and as a result, the Lord causes a huge earthquake that rocks the very foundations of the prison (see also 4:31).

7. Verses 27-30 – On discovering all the cell doors open, the jailor obviously assumed that all those under his charge had escaped and he would be held responsible (see 12:19). Yet none of the prisoners left! The jailor wanted to know how he could be saved and turned to those people who had been beaten and locked in prison and asked them for the answer to the big question of life.

8. Verses 31-34 – Even before Paul and Silas could baptise him, the jailor showed extraordinary hospitality towards these men, taking them from the prison to his own home to wash their wounds, showing the gifts of service and experiencing the joy of the Holy Spirit. The jailor was saved from death in more ways than one.

9. Verses 35-40 – By insisting on such a public exit from the city, Paul is not thinking of his own reputation as much as he is thinking of the reputation of the gospel and the security of the new believers.

10. Verses 11-40 – Lydia was born again and now had church meetings at her home. The slave girl was free, perhaps in more ways than one and the jailor and his whole household had received God's grace in Jesus Christ. All this was as a result of Paul and Silas talking to people they met about Jesus, whatever their own circumstances.

Acts 20:13-38

1. Verses 13-17 – Despite being the cause of a riot in Ephesus, Paul appears not to be reluctant to visit again because of concerns over his own safety. Rather, he is concerned that if he were to visit again, he would end up staying a long while!

2. Verses 18-21 – Paul's life style was one of humility, tears, and consistent and unashamed proclamation of the gospel both to large groups and in houses despite very difficult trials. The heart of his message to everyone, whether Jew or Gentile was the same – repent, turn to God and have faith in the Lord Jesus.

3. Verses 22-24 – Paul knows that hardships and prison await him almost everywhere he goes and he is sure that this will be the case in Jerusalem where he has been in trouble before (9:29). Yet his overriding concern is that he may complete the task the Lord Jesus himself gave him, the task of telling people about the grace of God.

4. Verses 25-27 – Paul considered the lives of people to be his responsibility to some extent until he has told them the good news of Jesus. This sort of attitude is by no means unique to Paul. The Old Testament prophets adopted the same attitude (see for example Ezekiel 33:1-9).

5. Verses 28-31 – Paul urges those who were to be responsible for the care of believers that they should be shepherds of those in their care. This role would be difficult, not least because there were people who opposed the work and wanted to see believers turn away from their trust in Jesus. Some of these wicked teachers would be people from within the church itself and Paul seems to have taught these many times, with tears, over the three years he was with them.

6. Verses 32-35 – Paul had lived a life of service, of hard work and of concern for the needy in particular, just as his Saviour had done. Like Jesus, Paul was not concerned about physical possessions and saw them more as a way of helping others rather than items to keep and hoard.

7. Verses 36-38 — Paul may sometimes be thought of as a difficult man to get on with and there are those who read his letters and are somewhat put off by him as a person. Yet the Ephesians elders were clearly deeply saddened by the thought that they would never see Paul again.

8. Verses 13-38 — This passage is one of the best places to turn for a list of the qualities and the duties that are to be desired and expected of those in church leadership. Such leadership is not limited to Vicars, Pastors, Bishops and the like. Christian leadership can be a Sunday school teacher, a parent, a home group leader or anyone who can exert influence over other Christians. This ultimately will include most of us.

BookbyBook

Study 9   Bible Answers

Acts 22:30-23:35

1. Verses 30 – On his missionary journeys, Paul has been free to go almost where he wants, yet since his arrival in Jerusalem we have not read of one convert. Paul has been on the back foot, having to defend himself and seems to have been pushed from pillar to post. The commander has failed to obtain a clear view of what Paul's accusers were so concerned about. He had asked the crowd in 21:33-34 with no luck and had considered torture. However he couldn't use this tactic on a Roman citizen, so now he turns to the religious leaders in search for an answer.

2. Verses 1-5 – Paul began by effectively telling the High Priest and all the Sanhedrin that he was right and they were all wrong. Paul simply says, "This news I am telling you about Jesus of Nazareth is the will of God." In striking Paul, the High Priest is doing the very opposite of Paul and acting in a way contrary to the way of God and Paul points this out to him.

3. Verses 6-8 – Knowing that this notion was an issue that divided even the hierarchy of the religious leaders, Paul forces them to think about this and presents the reality of Jesus to them. The Sadducees seem to be predominantly materialistic in their outlook, not accepting the existence of anything in the so-called "spiritual" world.

4. Verses 9-10 – Far from being people who would act justly, love mercy and walk humbly with their God (Micah 6:8), these people had become little more than violent mindless bigots. Once again we find God's servant protected, not by God's "people" but by their enemies.

5. Verse 11 – Paul must have been deeply encouraged by the word from the Lord. The Lord chose not to release Paul from prison. Rather he told Paul that this trial was going to continue for a while yet and would end with Paul speaking about Jesus in the very heart of the Roman Empire.

6. Verses 12-16 — On one hand we have the Lord, standing beside Paul and giving him strength to face what lies ahead. On the other hand we have the Jewish people, joining together to try and murder one man who threatened their way of life. This was Paul's life or theirs. What they failed to see was the hand of the Lord in all this. This was still Jesus, continuing his acts in the world.

7. Verses 17-22 — Claudias Lysias, the commander has now rescued Paul on four occasions in the last three chapters (the other three being 21:33-34, 22:22-29, 23:10). The Living God, who works everything together for the good of those who love him, knew exactly what he was doing. (See Isaiah 10:5, Proverbs 21:1).

8. Verses 23-30 — It appears that Lysias considers the matter now to be getting out of his control but is serious enough to refer "up the chain" to his boss.

9. Verses 31-35 — Paul had been told that this would be his role at his conversion (9:15) and he maybe wondered how he would reach people in such high positions. This was all still in the hands of the Lord who directing events from the heavenly throne room.

10. Verses 22:30-23:35 — Despite the fact that Paul is in a very different situation here to some of his previous encounters, Paul is still fulfilling his duty before God and is still taking every opportunity to speak to people about Jesus. As Paul is faithful to the Lord, so the Lord is faithful to him.

Acts 28:11-31

1. Verses 11-14 — Everything seems to have conspired to prevent Paul arriving at Rome. It clearly was an important part of the Lord's plan for Paul to be in Rome. Eventually finding some believers in Puteoli must have been a great source of encouragement for Paul and given him strength for the last leg of his journey.

2. Verses 15-16 — We are not told in Acts who was responsible for first taking the gospel to Rome, but we do know that there were visitors from Rome in Jerusalem on the day of Pentecost (Acts 2:10). The fact that Paul was allowed to live with only one guard shows us that he was not considered a threat and he had proved a number of times, especially on the boat, that he was not one to escape.

3. Verses 17-18 — After calling the leaders together, Paul explains that it was the Jews in Rome who had arrested him, even though he had done nothing that contradicted Jewish law. This was important because Paul wanted to share the same message with these hearers and needed them to know there was nothing for them to fear.

4. Verses 19-20 — Paul felt compelled to appeal to Caesar in order both to provide the largest possible sign that his message was not breaking any law, and also because the Lord had told him he was going to Rome. Paul considers himself to be in chains in connection with the hope of the very men stood in front of him.

5. Verses 21-22 — It is rather surprising that the Jerusalem Jews haven't got their most wanted man up on posters all over the place. Paul is able to start with a clean slate and present the message to people who were already anxious to hear Paul's message because it was being talked about, as a sect, everywhere.

6. Verses 23-24 — Of course Paul couldn't travel to them, but they didn't have to travel to him — they chose to. It is reminiscent of the crowds who fled the cities to hear John the Baptist all the way out in the wilderness (Mark 1:5).

7. Verses 25-28 – In particular, Paul's quote from Isaiah 6 was very hard hitting. He told Jews that the very scriptures they studied stated that they themselves would not hear the message. In stating that God's message was being presented to the Gentiles, Paul was effectively saying that if the Jewish leaders in front of him didn't respond, they would miss out on the work of God across the whole world.

8. Verses 30-31 – There is clearly no urgency on the part of Caesar's court to try Paul. He boldly preaches the kingdom of God and the truth about Jesus. Notice that many people came to him, as his mission boundaries were the confines of his house. Paul just can't help talking to people about Jesus (Ephesians 6:19-20, Philippians 1:14, 4:22).

9. Verses 11-31 – It appears he wrote at least three letters to Christians churches whilst in prison in Rome (see above references and Colossians 4:3, 18). It is fitting for the book to end here, without a real "full stop" because the continuing Acts of Jesus in all the nations hasn't reached a full stop either, yet. We have our role to play being witnesses to the risen Lord Jesus Christ to the ends of the earth.